TRAVELING
WITHOUT MOVING

TRAVELING WITHOUT MOVING

Essays from a Black Woman

Trying to Survive in America

TAIYON J. COLEMAN

UNIVERSITY OF MINNESOTA PRESS

MINNEAPOLIS   LONDON

The Publication History on pages 151–53 gives original and previous publication history for writings in this book.

Copyright 2024 by Taiyon J. Coleman

Published by the University of Minnesota Press
111 Third Avenue South, Suite 290
Minneapolis, MN 55401-2520
http://www.upress.umn.edu

ISBN 978-1-5179-1329-8 (pb)

Library of Congress record available at https://lccn.loc.gov/2024000289

Printed in the United States of America on acid-free paper

The University of Minnesota is an equal-opportunity educator and employer.

30 29 28 27 26 25 24   10 9 8 7 6 5 4 3 2 1

For Emmanuel, Shose, Ellykunda, and Mirai

Contents

Introduction

Mind the Gap

Memory was given to man for some wise purpose. The past is . . . the mirror in which we may discern the dim outlines of the future and by which we may make them more symmetrical.

—Frederick Douglass, *Narrative of the Life of Frederick Douglass: An American Slave Written by Himself,* 1884

The first time I noticed the Mind the Gap signs, I was taking a six-week language and literature study abroad course in London in the mid-1990s. A group of fellow students and I were standing on the Underground, or Tube, platform, waiting for the next train. In the city of London for the first time, I was seemingly amazed and impressed at how clever, simple, and thoughtful this transit message was regarding all the known, possible, and imagined dangers of a misstep—intentional or not—and falling into the abyss of the train's gap, which often resulted in serious injury and death.

At the time, memories of growing up on the South Side of Chicago and taking the L, Chicago's train system that runs elevated, under, and above ground, were there for comparison, but my single mother's relentless messages of staying away from Chicago's Metra's overpass train tracks and her matter-of-fact stories of Black kids playing on the train tracks and dying from electrocution or being hit by a speeding train never crossed my mind.[1]

When I read the Mind the Gap messages that day in London, my memories from riding Chicago L trains were of buying neatly packed plastic bags of fruit from elderly women standing on the L platforms for a dollar, but I didn't then remember my mother yanking me away from its edge, her warnings that people can push you over right before the train comes, that some people actually jump from the train's platform on purpose—and her own brush with death from a Chicago L train line.

Like clockwork, my mother picked us up each weekday from the babysitter, our next-door neighbor, by six in the evening. That Friday night in 1977, my mother, a single mother without a car, was late, and my sisters and I were the last to be picked up. Even as a child sitting in front of the TV news that night while waiting for my mother to walk through the babysitter's door, I didn't understand all the possibilities of what her lateness meant. It was only until my mother arrived many hours later that she would tell us her story.

When my mother arrived at the State and Lake L platform that day, like she did every weekday in time to catch the train that would get her to the 95th and Dan Ryan Station, the conductor, who usually holds the door open for any stragglers running up the stairs, stuck their head out the window, looked at her, and closed the train doors right in front of her face leaving her alone on the platform. It would be the last train to leave the State and Lake station that evening heading south to get my mother home until after the historic accident. According to *Chicago Tribune* journalist Elizabeth Greiwe:

---

1. See Richard Wronski, "Metra Train Deaths Force Police to Step Up Enforcement, Vigilance," *Chicago Tribune*, August 23, 2021.

It wasn't clear at first what had caused the crash. The Lake–Dan Ryan train had turned the corner to pull into the station at State and Lake. [The train] . . . hit something after coming around the curve at the corner of Lake Street and Wabash Avenue. . . . After a "quiet thump," the first two train cars started to wobble. Slowly, the back of the first car lifted into the air and then crashed into the street twenty feet below, dragging three other cars with it. [More than] . . . 160 were injured, and eleven people were killed.[2]

An L train would fall from the elevated downtown Chicago Loop train track, and just like that, a quiet thump as Greiwe described it, my mother's possible injury and death (there were eleven others not so lucky), by an infrastructure, a necessary institutional structure needed for travel, employment, and income, a gap, a same L train moving in a different direction, were seemingly and arbitrarily avoided or narrowly escaped.

I couldn't tell you then, and I can't tell you now, if there were any signs on Chicago train platforms during my childhood alerting me of the dangers of the gaps. I couldn't tell you if my mother was aware of her danger or the significance of her danger as my memory recalls her own reactions and retelling of her experience, her story. It seems that by the time my memories had caught up to me in the 1990s on that London train platform, I had accepted those very real and metaphorical gaps of danger as a normal part of my life and the cost for being able to travel, of being able to move in this, my life. So much so that I couldn't recognize the dangers enough to even be fearful or even recognize them as such. It was only as I worked to write these words with the intent to both

2. Elizabeth Greiwe, "The 'L' Crash of 1977: 'A Slow-Motion Horror,'" *Chicago Tribune*, May 11, 2019.

introduce and house this collection of recursive essays written over my experiences and memories of more than two decades that I can remember the dangers of public transportation, the dangers of life as a Black woman in the United States of America, and the L trains from my childhood.

I had normalized the gaps and dangers of my constructed identity of my lived experiences in order to exist, to survive, and to make sense of the world in the past and present moments. Standing on that London platform in the 1990s was a memory recall obscured with active escape and survival.

How do the legacies of institutional and structural racism create quiet but huge gaps in our lives and lived experiences that we, as oppressed identities and bodies working daily to thrive and sometimes just to survive, get caught up into or narrowly miss every day? How as an act of survival, mercy, and resilience do we pull through our encounters with these gaps and live to arrive in safe, creative, and critical mental and physical spaces where we can use memory and self-reflection to recall and construct meaning and deconstruct White supremacy?

Today, it's a greater memory, still not complete or perfect, but a fuller picture that works to include my escapes, catastrophes, and the narrow navigations of the dangers along the way with compassion, empathy, humor, and humanity.

• • •

When I decided to complete my college degree in the 1990s, I started at a community college in Des Moines, Iowa, after having dropped out for more than four years. My cool composition teacher drove a red Pontiac Fiero, and she shared with the class that she had just recently been diagnosed with a condition that required that she walk with a cane. I was apprehensive about taking a college writing class because I had big-time failed my freshman composition class as a new incoming university student. That big juicy F in my composition course was the significant event that triggered the domino effect that eventually led to me dropping out of school altogether.

African American, female, poor, and a first-generation college student, I remember going to college after high school because that is what everyone else did. It was expected of me from day one of my twelve-year Chicago parochial and segregated education. I was the first generation born a year after the assassination of Martin Luther King, and I was expected to be the fulfillment of those generations of struggle and what the United States thought was change and promise, i.e., equality.

I was among the generations of Black kids growing up in Chicago in the '70s and '80s who were two generations removed from Mississippi and Arkansas, and our parents and their parents had sacrificed so much for us to have and to do better. Although I was one of five kids raised by a single parent and poor on the South Side of Chicago, I really believed that I had no excuse or reason for dropping out of college when it happened. And when it happened, it happened in *movie slow motion*, and the Universe was very clear in telling me that I had really fucked some shit up.

I remember, now that I am at a seemingly safe distance, that I really didn't understand what was going on. I was trying so hard to go through the motions of achieving educational success as prescribed for me, barely keeping my head above water. For someone like me who never learned how to swim until after I went to graduate school, the analogy of trying to swim in deep water when you can't swim but are expected to, tricked into believing that you can, and have never been taught, embeds the fear, frustration, desperation, and confusion that I felt over the twenty-five years of experiences that my essays span.

When I was in high school, a group of me and my neighborhood friends snuck into a school swimming pool. I didn't know how to swim, so I stayed in the shallow end of the pool. When we were leaving, my friend asked me why I didn't swim in the deep end.

"I can't swim," I told him.

He didn't believe me, and he picked me up and threw me into the seventeen feet of water in the pool's deep end.

Luckily, my body popped back to the surface. I splashed and clawed my way to the pool's ledge to pull myself out of the water. I remember ugly-crying and sobbing and my friend profusely apologizing. He just couldn't believe that I had never learned how to swim. We left the pool that day, and we, I, acted like I didn't almost drown. As a Black woman navigating historically and predominantly White institutions, structures, and spaces, my life has been like that moment in the pool.

For the years when I was a college dropout, I worked and volunteered at a nonprofit community radio station in Des Moines. I had a talk show where I read and talked about local current events, African American history, and sometimes read books by African American authors: Toni Morrison's *Beloved*, *The Autobiography of Malcolm X*, and Lucille Clifton's *Good Woman*, which was a gift from a White listener.

For a while I thought that my life without a college degree wasn't half-bad. I was able to make a living, read and talk about books, and serve my community. I got to see MC Hammer, Boyz II Men, and Whitney Houston in concert; I had a nice one-bedroom apartment in an old Victorian house attic. Chicago was a six-hour drive away, so I could travel home anytime I wanted to, but I was far enough away that my family couldn't regularly visit me. During that time I often thought to myself, "I could make that not finishing college thing work." Until it didn't.

At one of my really good jobs that came with a cubicle, a bi-weekly paycheck, and health insurance, I naively told my boss during a performance review, after I had already been promoted three times in the company, that I could see myself doing their management job when they asked how I saw my future in the company. My boss, who was White and the manager, didn't have a college degree, and at the time neither did I. Six months later I was fired. Set this on repeat.

So as I write in the essay "You Can Miss Me with That, 'Cause Plantations Were Diverse, Too," when my community college composition teacher told me that I was a writer after she read some of my first-person essays, I didn't believe her. She had tasked the class with writing first-person essay assignments, and the only words that would come for me were the words that traveled me back to my childhood growing up on the South Side of Chicago. It was as if the memories were lined up ready to go and basically telling me that my only path forward was to revisit, see, analyze, and integrate my past in order to understand and see my present, in order to move forward, and to hopefully live, survive, and thrive.

Through writing, I had to return to and swim in those waters, insidious placid pools, where I regularly tried not to drown. The notions of past, present, and future shifted for me in those moments of revisiting the past through writing memories juxtaposed to my then-present identities, knowledge, and experiences. Those early college dropout essays taught me that I had traveled physically in time, space, and location for almost twenty-four years, but I had not moved. Although I couldn't know it then, writing would become *the* vehicle for me to make sense of the incongruencies of my experiences and the world; it would become a way for me to think and to survive to help myself and, hopefully, others.

I completed my community college composition class that semester with an A and eventually returned to the first institution where I first started college and then dropped out. I declared English literature as my major, and I have never looked back.

Well, only through writing.

. . .

This collection of essays is not comprehensive in that it is not a linear autobiography. The essays represent recursive remembered experiences that I have had from childhood through the twenty-first century and are an attempt to tell and understand my story within the larger structural dynamics, which affected and affect my present experiences.

Many writing acquisition teachers believe that writing is a certain way of thinking, and that critical thinking, discovery, and creativity are recursive and not linear. Things seem to not make sense and be connected in order for us, through writing, to discover in fact that it's all connected and that by connecting the dots, the spaces and meanings, possibly memory, we can make our writing and what we want to communicate comprehensive.

My essays span from early memories of when I first realized I wanted to be a writer at age eight, consider the contradictions of being Black and Catholic throughout my memories, experiences of being a Black female student in a predominantly White graduate program, experiences of racial rejection, heartbreak, infant loss, motherhood, and home ownership for more than a decade in a state that has the largest racial disparities in the nation, to my experiences as an "educated" professional taking hits at the intersections of oppression, gender, and racism, and the challenges of teaching writing and trying to keep my heart, empathy, and compassion while Black.

For me recursive memory and writing are like a dog that circles the ground until it makes itself comfortable and safe before sitting. Some canine experts call this circling behavior an act of "self-preservation and protection, [which] . . . is protective of the members of the pack . . . and identifies [a canine's] place in the pecking order of the pack."[3] They even go on to say that it is an instinctual way to look out for stragglers, a way to make sure that all the members of the pack stay together, a way to close the gaps in their journeys so that everyone makes it home and everyone can stay alive.

Somehow, with each trip back into my past, compelled by a desire to better understand my present moment, the impact of that past upon my present becomes clearer. It is not necessarily a right or a correct thing; it is a way of being, and a way for me to make sense of the world. A way to express compassion and empathy. It is a way to make art. Possibly, an attempt to share with you the way that I see and move through the world. I understand that in this way I privilege the written word, memory, and perception in my essays, for at least now, along with my heart, writing is the only thing that I trust.

---

3. Ryan Llera and Lynn Buzhardt, "Why Dogs Turn around before Lying Down," VCA Animal Hospitals website. https://vcahospitals.com/know-your-pet/why-dogs-turn-around -before-lying-down

The Thenar Space

When I was just eight years old, a "thousand injuries of my . . .
[auntie] I had borne as I best could, but when . . . [she] ven-
tured upon insult, I vowed revenge."

—Edgar Allan Poe, "The Cask of Amontillado" (1846)

"You're too stupid to ever write about anything" is what my aunt-
ie laughed and said to me in response. I had announced in my
grandmother's house at the dinner table that I was going to write
a book, my first novel. From her calling me stupid to teasing me
about my weight and laughing about my loud asthmatic snoring
in the middle of the night, I was determined to write about all the
injustices that I had suffered at the hands of my wicked auntie with
her skinny-ass Jordache jeans and an early 1980s feathered haircut.

Although she was my mother's baby sister, she was only six
years older than me, and she viewed me as her nemesis. Earlier
that morning, she hung the multicolored living room rug out to
dry on the wire clothesline directly facing me and all my neighborhood friends, including the one brown boy that I liked as we played
run-in-bases in the adjacent yard. As the area rug dried, a round
darkness demarcated the space where I had an accident as I slept on
the floor pallet the night before. (At my grandma's house, I wasn't

allowed to sleep in a bed or on her couch.) Hanging that carpet out to dry announced to all my friends that I wet the bed, and like the narrator Montresor in Poe's "The Cask of Amontillado," I vowed to take vengeance, a writer's payback, with the utmost impunity against my auntie for her insult. I would write a novel telling about her evil ebony Black ass.

During the month of June over that summer of my eighth year, I dug through my grandma's green-flowered couch cushions like a Peabody coal miner searching for the daily coins that my papa let slip nightly from his drunken pants pockets. With my shiny pilfered money, I made a bike trip to the Sparta Pharmacy. I purchased Bottle Caps, Lemonheads, Jolly Ranchers (we called them wine candy), a big shiny black blinder, a Bic blue pen, and the biggest freaking packet of white notebook paper that I could find. I think it was a paper packet of one hundred pages. I know. It was so lovely. I still get excited when I encounter empty writing paper today. Once home, I ran into my grandparents' house, and like any serious author, I sat down to use their coffee table to ceremoniously prepare my writing materials. Even at eight years old, I believed that procedure and process were everything.

I stuffed all my candy into my sweaty gray-white bra distributing it evenly between my breasts, lest I be subjected to my big sister's finders-keepers-losers-weepers law. I know I was only eight years old, but I was a big Black girl, and yes, I was wearing a bra, and no, it was not a training bra.

I took the blue Bic pen out of the store bag and I placed it gently on the coffee table next to my grandma's hoarder stack of *People* magazines. Jesus himself help you if you tried to throw just one away, especially the ones that were at least five years old. My momma always wrote with a blue pen in her checkbook, in her word-circle puzzle books, and on little sheets of white paper that I occasionally found crumbled up on top of the kitchen garbage can where she had obsessively, what seemed to me at the time, added and subtracted the same numbers over and over again in order to arrive at a budget number greater than zero. I wanted to be like Momma in any way that I could, but according to my grandma my skin was too dark and I was too hardheaded, and as a result hard pressed, to get any lighter. During my summers in Sparta, Illinois, I didn't do a good job of taking grandma's sage advice to stay out of the sun and to always wear a pair of shoes on my feet. They didn't carry skin lightener cream at the Sparta Pharmacy, but they did sell single blue Bic pens. So if my skin could not be as light as my Momma's, at least my writing ink color would be just like hers. Grandma didn't know anything about genetics back then and neither did I; to her, I had fucked up my skin color (too dark), my weight (too heavy), my hair (too nappy), my height (too tall), my mouth (too loud), and my feet (too large).

No worries. There was room for Grandma in the retribution novel narrative, too.

Removing the plastic wrap from the notebook paper, I sifted the stack of white paper with red lines directly on top of the coffee table (to even it out, of course) before placing the paper inside the black binder. I oscillated between holding the stack of paper up to my nose and breathing deeply of its woodsy scent and pounding it back on the table. The steady, hard, and loud whacks of tightly held one hundred pieces of paper repeatedly hitting my grandma's wood coffee table, recently polished with asthma-inducing Pledge furniture polish, reverberated throughout her shotgun house and made my heart race in anticipation of my first written words.

"What the hell is that goddamn racket?" my grandma yelled at me from the kitchen.

I didn't answer.

"Olon!" she called for my papa trying to figure out what the hell was going on. He had already escaped the house to Micheaux's, the local watering hole on the west end of town via his red riding lawn mower at about six miles an hour. The sun would fall before Papa would return to find my grandma asleep in her room, me on a pallet on the living room floor, and him on the couch for what was left of the night. I don't think the Sparta police gave out RLMWUIs (Riding a Lawn Mower While Under the Influence) back then.

"Cut that shit out, girl!" Grandma followed up with an even louder voice when she didn't get a response from my papa, and it didn't even phase me.

I had one hundred new and even empty white sheets of paper with a new blue Bic pen awaiting a rendezvous with a new black shiny binder, and I was going to write my goddamn novel. I was in heaven, and not even my grandma's shouted threats of a fresh green tree switch with my full name written-all-up-on-it torn from the front-yard oak tree could take this moment away from me. The second chapter of my novel was going to be solely devoted to grandma's mean ass in detail, and remember, the first chapter was destined for my auntie (aka Fortunato).[1]

The last piece for my materials assembly, the shiny black binder, lay flat and open with its even shinier metal clips in the middle. Leaning over the coffee table I placed a hand on each end clip of the binder, I pressed the metal tabs, and the circle clips popped open. Smiling wide, I grabbed the pack of paper like I used to grab my two-year-old brother who I raised from a baby, and I lined up the notebook paper circles with the open circular metal clips. I replaced my hands on each of the clips and pressed the tabs. The tabs clicked into space and closed.

It took a second for me to realize that my skin, the fleshy web-

---

1. Montresor cleverly uses Fortunato's hubris against him and outwits Fortunato in the catacombs where Montresor buries Fortunato alive. I in no way advocate that writers use violence and/or violence against family members in this, my essay. I am using Poe's short story as a writing metaphor and making an attempt at levity. As a writer, I subscribe to the saying that the "pen is mightier than the sword."

bing between my left index finger and thumb, which I now know is anatomically called the *thenar,* was shooting daggers through my left hand and up the left side of my body. (The Greek root, *thenein,* means to strike, as in the palm part of the hand one would use to strike something or someone.) I looked down, and I realized that I had caught my hand inside the lock of the binder's metal circle clips. For a moment I was stuck, as I couldn't pull my flesh from the metallic circle's hold or I risked tearing a complete hole into my skin. Breathing deeply, I used my right hand to press down on the left tab of the binder and pop!—all the metal circle clips opened.

"Well, ain't that shit a bitch," one of my grandma's most popular catch phrases, ran through my mind, and I was able to gently remove the flesh between my thumb and my index finger from the Death Star grip of the binder's metal ring.[2] Small, red, almost black dots dripped across my fresh white paper before I could place my hand inside my mouth to suck the blood in order to solve the next writing challenge facing me.

To conserve paper, I decided to write on both sides of the notebook paper because I didn't know when I would be able to raise enough couch coins for the purchase of more paper, and I just knew that I had a lot of shit to write, because in my eight-year-old mind these people had been doing me dirty for eight fucking years too many. There were not enough small bags of spicy hard pork rinds and bottles of homemade root beer in the world to soothe my mind, body, and spirit of their perpetual slights.

Steve Perry (from Journey) and his heartfelt "Don't Stop Believin'" played in the background from the ajar door of my auntie's

---

2. A reference to George Lucas's *Star Wars* and the Death Star seemed appropriate here, as in this moment I truly understood what the Force meant. I was trying to work in the light, but clearly, my grandma and auntie were using their Force for the dark side, and my hand injury was the result. My real parents were dead, I was in the wrong fucking family, and I just needed to wait for my Ben Obi-Wan Kenobi, C-3PO, and R2-D2 to show up, and then things would be right with the world.

bedroom where her brand-new '80s blue stereo set with matching speakers sat directly in front of her queen size bed. As the metallic taste of blood from my left hand soothed me, I used my right hand to start my retribution masterpiece and oscillated between writing with my right hand and picking and eating my candy out of my sweaty bra, as my grandma repeatedly complained that the house thermostat for the air conditioner was set on hell.

I wrote sitting on the couch in the living room in Sparta for what seemed like hours in front of the TV. *The Young and the Restless* had started, and by the time I came to the bottom of the back of the first page, the soap opera was over, my left hand had stopped bleeding, my candy from my bra was all gone, I seemed to have exhausted my injustices, and my right hand was severely cramping.

Today, no matter how hard I try, I can't remember anything after that moment, and I don't ever recall returning back to that shiny black notebook to finish my handwritten novel. I do, however, still carry the pain from all the bad things that my auntie and grandma said about me and did to me. When those memories become really bad, I now know that writing, believing in myself, and having the courage to tell and write my stories were and are a powerful weapon that no one, not even my grandma and my auntie, can ever take away from me. Of course, I hope that my craft of good writing has grown from simple Edgar Allan Poe reckoning and justice stories to narratives of the human condition with the complex and creative ability to weave empathy and compassion into individual and specific characters and their infinite conflicts that work to resonate beyond the personal.

I hope that with craft, empathy, and compassion, my writing grew to tell beautiful and tragic tales of what possibly happened to a young Black girl born in the 1930s in a small rural town on the Mason–Dixon line that could make her grow to be so mean and ugly to her own children and grandchildren, and my writing now explores the social and family dynamics of generational addiction, racial oppression, sexual abuse, and poverty that easily turned the soft rock of the '80s, a featured haircut, and a pair of brand-new Jordache jeans into a stone-cold inhumane bitch before the age of sixteen.

• • •

So what does this have to do with alternative approaches to creative writing?

As a writer, I learned early in my life from the people closest to me, my family members, that writing and being a writer would be an extremely challenging thing for a poor Black girl from Chicago to do and be. It's one thing for Frederick Douglass to write about the curse of new knowledge upon acquiring literacy while enslaved.[3] Juxtapose this with me actually living—in "free times"— being literate and still having to act against the silencing by my family members, society, culture, and institutions as a woman writer of color.[4] Negative experiences have first and foremost come from my family and the struggles of a belief in myself, which are affected and compounded, like really high interest on bad debt, by structural and cumulative racism and sexism, manifested at a micro, individual level. As a black female writer, I have had to fight against my family, community, self, and institution while writing simultaneously. In this vein, my literary culture is a proud culture

3. In his autobiography, Douglass speaks of the ironic epiphany that literacy brings to his condition of slavery and ignorance. Once he can read, he learns how enslaved he is mentally and physically, and ironically he also becomes more dangerous as a literate slave because his agency increases.

4. Patricia Hill Collins argues that "the convergence of all these factors . . . the suppression of Black women's voice by dominant groups, Black women's struggles to work within the confines of norms of racial solidarity, and the seeming protections offered by a culture of dissemblance influences yet another factor shaping patterns of silence." Collins, *Black Feminist Thought* (New York: Routledge, 2009), 135.

of struggling against silencing to result in the power, art, agency, beauty, and self-actualization that comes from speaking and writing in spite of.[5]

Overcoming my negative writing experiences is a daily practice of consistent writing and self-love through individual work and effort and community. The rules for my craft are simple: just read and write when and where you can about what you want. In *On Writing*, Stephen King says that "if you want to be a writer, you must do two things above all others: read a lot and write a lot. There's no way around these two things." Turn off those negative self-voices, those negative people, and negative situations and do the positive you, which is believing in yourself and in your writing through direct action: reading, writing, and loving yourself—challenges and all!

As a partnered woman with three kids and a full-time job, I try to not write when my hair is on fire, and I am always working to develop a routine practice. In lieu of a practice that may be challenging in the face of prioritized responsibilities like kids, work, life, etc., I have joined writing groups and make contracts with my writing friends in my writing, creative, and artistic communities to challenge one another and keep ourselves on task by being accountable to others. Ultimately, my goal as a writer is just to produce writing that tells my story and has utility for readers; I want to always connect outside of myself and my world to the equally valuable worlds and experiences of others. In this way I am connected, connecting, and never alone. As a prose and poetry writer, I would like to leave you with a writing exercise that uses an object to facilitate the creative and objective writing experience, which often leads to discovery of new and exciting writing content.

---

5. See Zora Neale Hurston, "Characteristics of Negro Expression"; Langston Hughes, "The Negro Artist and the Racial Mountain"; and Richard Wright, "Blueprint for Negro Writing"—all included in *The Norton Anthology of African American Literature*, 2nd ed., ed. Henry Louis Gates Jr. and Nellie Y. McKay (New York: Norton, 2004).

I find that writing about a seemingly arbitrary object from one's own memory tied to other details of that memory helps to balance the emotions that can sometimes be overwhelming and obscure the creative craft and component needs of writing and the story itself for readers. Sometimes good writing is intentional, but most often times it is an act of discovery while writing.

In *The Triggering Town*, Richard Hugo believes that the best writing resides within a trigger or a detail, which is usually a concrete image that the writer discovers in the early drafts of their writing. Hugo believes that the trigger in the writing, like a light in the dark, signals the writer regarding the direction and development that their writing content and structure should take. The *vehicle* in writing is the concrete detail and/or image that can carry infinite themes and meanings to the readers. The *tenor* contains the infinite themes and meanings carried to the reader through the vehicle of the writing. Put differently, the vehicle is like a car that can carry the passenger (tenor) in a narrative. The value of your own writing often resides in the irony and tension between details of the past (revisited memories and feelings) knowledge of the writer (subject) juxtaposed to the hindsight (present details) contemporary view and knowledge of the writer and their readers.

Fool's Gold

"Hey! Stop running. Come here and let me look at you, girl," my great-aunt Reola said.

Aunt Reola was my papaw's big sister. There was only one nursing home because Sparta, Randolph County, Illinois, was a small historic town, part of the Underground Railroad, with only one of everything, and Aunt Reola lived in the one convalescent home.[1] On Sundays my papaw would go get Aunt Reola in the morning, and she would spend the day with us, sitting quietly in my grandma's green chair, watching Westerns and WWE matches on the big floor-model TV with my papaw and eating supper with us before he would return her to the nursing home.

"Hi," I said, as I entered the house from the front porch while the ripe smells of recently picked tomatoes, green beans, and cucumbers waiting patiently in wooden baskets for canning filled my nose. I was thirsty, and like a bullet I had entered my grandma's quasi shotgun home from playing running bases outside in the August sun. I was out of breath but showing the right amount of respect for my elders as I tried to continue skipping past Aunt Reola and her words, making sure that I didn't run over her diabetic feet. My older sister and I were making the best of our last few weeks

---

1. Ironically, the town's other claim to fame is that the movie *In the Heat of the Night*, starring Sidney Poitier, was mostly filmed there.

visiting our grandparents before our mother would drive down from Chicago to get us back to the city in enough time to start the new school year.

• • •

When I was a little kid, I thought that one of the coolest things in the world was being able to pee in a blue water toilet on a moving bus.

While I was middle-school age, my single mother shipped me and my older sister by Greyhound bus from the Ninety-fifth Street and Dan Ryan Station to East St. Louis once school let out for the summer. My strong beautiful mother turned scandalous wife of a too dark Black city slicker by gossip and subsequent divorce was convinced that my sister and I running the dusty red chat-lined roads without sidewalks in the small town of her birth would be much safer than spending latchkey 1980s summers alone in our South Side Chicago home while she went to work every day.

With our cold fried chicken sandwiches and cans of red pop[2] rolled precisely in grocery store brown paper bags and relentless warnings of not to talk to or sit next to any strangers and not to sit directly on the bus toilet when we went to the bathroom, we would be met by our grandparents at the Greyhound station in East St. Louis, a city one Mississippi River east of the 1820 Missouri Compromise, as long as we arrived there "before dark"—my grandma's words.

After one hour of car driving deeper south into the Land of Lincoln on hilly meandering two-lane roads between wafts of manure, newly planted corn and soybean fields, and set back strip-pit lakes, when we finally crossed the Kaskaskia River, a tributary of the Mississippi River that separates the southern part of the state

---

2. Where I was born and raised on the South Side of Chicago, the word *red* was used to signify a flavor of a beverage or candy and also to describe a color.

from Missouri, into Randolph County, I knew that we had arrived at the place that was my summer home, my mother's and her people's home.

My grandparents' nineteenth-century home was in the small expatriate-named southern Illinois town of Sparta. Originally part of French Colonial Country from the very late seventeenth century, it became part of French Louisiana and then remained under British control until the American Revolution. Although it was known as a free state, African American slaves, as in many northern states and territories, were held in Illinois from the eighteenth century. Some of our family members, Black, White, German, and Indigenous, came to Illinois from the Carolinas, Louisiana, Missouri, Germany, and intersected in Randolph County.

My grandma's house had yellow siding and central air. From the front porch you could see the entire house in this order: the living room, the one bureau and bathroom hallway, and the green kitchen in the very back with two separate bedroom additions on its right side.

• • •

"Let me see you for a minute, girl," Aunt Reola said.

She grabbed my left arm stopping me in midstride. She smelled like peppermint chewing gum and coffee. I was surprised at how smooth her hands felt against my brown skin, as she ran them down my arm until she reached my hand, which forced me to turn my body to stand straight in front of hers. At eleven years old in 1981, I was a big girl. I was tall enough to face her, almost eye to eye, as I stood directly in front of Aunt Reola while she sat in the sofa chair. Next to her was a wooden side table with a lamp. She pulled me near the light so she could see me better.

Initially, I tried to resist and pull away, but gently she squeezed my hands touching all of my fingers one by one as she pulled me even closer to the bright light and to her face. Finally, realizing that strength did not have to hurt, I relaxed my body into hers and surrendered. Aunt Reola's glass-covered brown eyes, which seemed to be rimmed in blue mist, carefully studied my face for what seemed like forever as she smiled wide. Her hands were as soft as the words she spoke to me, like she had discovered a treasure chest of gold that only she could see.

"Do you know that you look just like my sister, little girl? She's been long gone now, but you have her same exact eyes. So big. So brown. So pretty. You look just like her," she emphasized each word with a shake of her hands in mine before gently bringing her hands to frame my chocolate chubby round face.

A rediscovered joy at experiencing a deep feeling thought forever lost emanated from Aunt Reola's face, and its realness made me uncomfortable. For a moment I believed that Aunt Reola, looking dead-straight at me, really believed if not fully felt that I was her actual sister.

"No," was the best response I had, as I really didn't know what else to say or do. Aunt Reola was one of the few family members on my mother's side who did not comment on my being and physical looks in terms of how much darker my skin was than my mother's, or how big my feet were because I did not like to wear shoes ever, or how fat I was.

I could count on one hand how many times I had met Aunt Reola. I knew that she and her brother, my papaw, were the last of their living siblings. Their family had made their way to southern Illinois from the Carolinas. As a kid I just thought that's how things were in everyone's families. Family members, especially elders and/or their ancestors, came from other places in the southern United States that folks didn't talk about; you were just described or designated by family elders as blue-black, black, red, red-bone, high-yellow, or passing and looking like those (them) peoples.[3] People in Sparta always told you who you looked like and who they thought you "was kin to" while looking at you all up in your face, carefully, before you were even allowed to tell them your name. You first name wasn't really that important; it was who your people were, who and what you looked like, who you were connected to, and from who and where you came out up from.

In Sparta, family members died young, and you were lucky to grow old and have all your teeth or be able to afford dentures if you did not have your teeth. The fact that my grandparents owned their own home that had an inside toilet (dating from after the birth of my oldest sister); central air, paid-for cable, a running car, and a set of dentures each—one for my grandma and one for my papaw— was the equivalent of having made it for them as Black people living in a small town in southern Illinois in the '70s and '80s.

While looking at me, Aunt Reola had this faraway look in her eyes, as if looking at me made her feel young, like a little girl again, and not an old brittle woman so incapable of taking care of herself that she had to live in a nursing home with total strangers without the companionship of her sister. As she watched me with great curiosity, almost like she was trying to convince herself that I was not her actual sister, I thought of all the fun she must have had with her sister, like I had with my sister when she wasn't being mean to me. I also thought of how much Aunt Reola must have loved and missed her sister, and I was ready for her to talk more about my dead great-aunt that I never had the opportunity to meet. But she said entirely something else.

"Like my sister, your eyes show too much, baby. You see too

---

3. Both my mother's and father's sides of the family were color-struck, like many families and people socialized within larger racialized U.S. American histories, identities, and experiences. As a result, colorism was a big part of my childhood and family experience, especially in determining physical and emotional value within the family.

much. I feel so sorry for you. You are too sensitive, and you will have to learn how not to show everything you think and feel through your face . . . through your eyes," she ended.

Aunt Reola's soft hands, brown like mine, left my face, touched my cornrow braids, and trailed down to their multicolored glass-beaded ends, finally journeying to my shoulders and back down my arms to tightly grab my hands again.

I remember feeling like it wasn't a real question or something that I could respond to. I felt awkward but so very curious at the same time. I knew I didn't understand the full meaning of Aunt Reola's words. I didn't understand her warning.

I thought that maybe Aunt Reola might have been making fun of me because I collected all the mine dollars that my papaw and uncles gave me. My papaw when he was younger and my uncles all worked in the coal mines, and they always brought home these mine dollars, pyrite sun, or "fool's gold," as my grandma called them. No one ever wanted the brass-colored mine dollars but me.

"Everything that glitter ain't gold," my grandma would say and follow it up with, "The shit's worthless!"

But I would keep the yellow and brassy colored metals and hide them. I thought then and still do that they were beautiful. Maybe this is what my aunt Reola was talking about. She saw how much interest I had in small things, and how that interest and my desire to have something I liked and loved brought me so much joy or pain, and I showed it. It was among the first lessons that nothing, even people that you come from and come from you, really belonged to you.

Now as an adult, I know that Aunt Reola saw me and felt sorry for me because she knew that I was the kid that saw, heard, and felt everything even when I didn't understand it all and when the adults thought that I wasn't looking, listening, or feeling. Aunt Reola knew that I was the kid that boldly looked at adults in the face, despite their threats of getting a fresh green tree switch to my bare brown legs. How did she know I was always the one who got in trouble for looking adults in the face, for always asking the wrong questions, or "being too grown and nosey"?

• • •

My father, who is one generation removed from Mississippi and Arkansas, tells the story, before my mother left him, of taking me and my sister to our neighborhood grocery store in Chicago. I was three years old, and we were waiting in the checkout line to pay for our food. There was a woman standing in front of us, and I was looking up at her. She had a dark brown birthmark that covered half of her face. My father says that I walked up to the lady, touched her hand, and asked her a very sincere and loud question in the way that only three-year-olds can.

"Does that thing on your face hurt? Can I touch it?"

"No. It doesn't hurt," the woman said simply.

My father snatched me up and apologized to the woman before I could find out if she was gonna let me touch her face.

When we arrived back home from the grocery store, my father sent me to my bedroom. He put away the food, and I got a whipping with my father's South Side Chicago belt instead of with a green Sparta tree switch.

"Do you want me to whip her again, Ron?" I heard my mother ask my father after he retold her what happened in the grocery store. I felt so betrayed. I thought one belt whipping was enough.

My father tells that story now with functional liquor and laughter. He says that as a Black man, an unemployed college dropout, a very young twentysomething father of two kids under the age of four living in Jim Crow Chicago in the seventies, and married to a Black Catholic woman without reliable and safe birth control, he was very embarrassed by my loudness, my impulsiveness, and my spirited inquisitiveness. According to my father, I didn't know how to act right. I didn't know my place.

As a mother of three children now, it is hard for me to ever imagine that a child asking smart questions and critically interacting with their environment is a bad thing—a thing so bad that it required punishment.

"You never stopped talking and asking questions," my father says.

Clearly I didn't get it. This was the man who had radically introduced me and my sister to *Sesame Street* and *The Electric Company* by the time I was three years old! What did he think was going to happen?

I now hold my father's story and others in me like hidden pieces of candy in my pocket or in the damp middle inside of my bra, adjacent to my heart, and I am waiting for the right time and space to take out, unwrap, taste, eat, and savor. With compassion, empathy, and working on "no judgment," I now know that my father was very afraid. He believed that he had to break me of my fearlessness. Like many parents generationally oppressed and living in de facto apartheid systems, my father believed he had to break me of asking critical questions. He believed he had to break me of trying to understand. He believed that he had to break me of trying to travel and move into the people, places, and spaces of interacting in the world, my world, and becoming me and being free.

Maybe this is what Aunt Reola saw in me on that late summer day in August.

• • •

I stood there in front of Aunt Reola. After a couple of seconds, I just felt awkward and wanted to go get a drink of water.

Now, as a writer who has aged, I can use my memory and words to return to that moment to see and understand more of what was there. I realize now that my soul's job has always been to look and try to see the past, the present, and the future and to use my experiences, my empathy, and my compassion to teach and to write, to record and bear witness to my family's and my ancestors' (human) experiences, as their lives and their abilities to survive, to thrive, and to love the best way they knew how were and are the very foundation and essence of my own life, making sense of my experiences and my existence.

In that way Aunt Reola, like many of my relatives and ancestors and their stories, were and are my best writing mentors.

How could I know that every interaction with my family members relative to their and my experiences, even the ones that I did not understand or enjoy, would become like a map, a trail of hot and spicy pork rinds or sock-it-to me cake crumbs, which they would and were leaving me, consciously and subconsciously?

The internal and personal. The external. The universal. The human.

Their stories, joy, pain, suffering, survival, oppression, exploitation, struggles, and anger among infinite emotions were the clues and coordinates to be able to return to one day if and when I have the courage to continue looking and seeing. If and when I have the discipline and commitment to continue writing and journeying along those lines, those maps, wherever it and they may take me. In that way, I am merely honoring my ancestors' doing what they did so that their legacies can continue, as their sacrifice and very defiance to survive, thrive, and love the best they knew how have afforded me an education, literacy, and my ability to purchase paper and pen—to write myself, my family, my ancestors, and us into existence, into freedom, and into humanity.

For what is the true value of believed gold to its owner that the world mistakes for and treats like a fool?

• • •

So when I start to create, to write, and to tell stories, I know that my ancestors are with me. It is a collaborative and cumulative process, and if I am worthy, I become a vessel to tell my stories and humbly understand that they are not just my stories. They are stories contributing to a larger collective that works to document and evidence the human and soul experience. But more important, I hope that they demonstrate beauty, empathy, compassion, respect, growth, and hopefully discovery, love, transformation, and humanity. Ideally, art.

Aunt Reola knew, if not directly or intuitively, that I was the looker, the watcher, the seer, the listener, the feeler, *the valuer,* the crier, the teller—*the fool.* The empath who felt, reordered, and continues to feel and record what interests me, what affects me, and what I can see and tell.

My ancestors mentored and *mused* me by trusting me with their words, their stories, their memories, and their love the best way that they could show it and tell it. As the proceeding generation, they had poured into me so that I could have better than they did, even if better was sleeping on the floor like they did. I slept on a floor with a warm pallet of thick blankets that my profanity-filled and green-tree-switch-swinging grandma made for me, and it was the softest bed that I ever have ever known.

My Aunt Reola saw all that in me. She seemed to know that I was that person in the family. She saw the storyteller in me, and while she clearly felt sorry for me, she also found some way to warn, affirm, soothe, and orient me.

I understood then from Aunt Reola's words that my brown eyes were not mine. They were a gift from her sister who I had never met or heard of, only that she had long died before I was born, like many of Papaw's family members. They are the eyes of a writer, sensitive, fractured, and obsessive in details and memory because my calling—vocation—is to first see and feel, recount, read, write, and speak the story in prose or poetry when, where, and how it feels and vibrates to me and through me.

If I do my job well, the story then documents that we and they exist and existed; live and lived; survive and survived; thrive and thrived; love and loved; and were and are so worthy. I am and we are human and have humanity. As a mentor, Aunt Reola affirmed all those qualities in me that the adults and others around me defined as bad. I now know that she saw it as a gift and calling. What greater mentor and muse can one have?

• • •

Susan Borders, "Sukey," a Black woman, was brought to live and work in the Sparta area along with her three sons as indentured servants, de facto slaves, by Sukey's White master, wealthy Randolph County landowner Andrew Borders, from the state of Georgia in the first half of the nineteenth century. Randolph County court records show that Sukey was indentured to work at the age of five to Borders, and Sukey's children were indentured to Borders also before the age of five, with her youngest son indentured at the age of six months. Once arriving in the Sparta area, Sukey traveled north on the Underground Railroad with her three children, Jarrot, Anderson, and Harrison, with the help of local White abolitionist William Hayes. Ultimately, Sukey's three children would be recaptured and returned to servitude to Andrew Borders. Jarrot would die in a farming accident, and her other two sons would remain enslaved. Sukey, a mother, would live the rest of her life free but without her three children.

When my mother died prematurely at the age of forty-nine, it took me years to go through the boxes of her personal belongings, and even twenty-six years later her boxes sit in my basement on utility shelves still unopened. The one box I did open is an old Lane cedar box. It is full of old pictures, many in black and white, and the ones in early color are old but still newer. Because the written dates and notes have faded with time on the back of the pictures, I don't recognize all the images, but I see hopeful wide smiles, pretty teeth, bright eyes, round cheeks—faces that are somewhat like mine, some more than others. However, it's not important that I know the people in the photographs, because they are important to me because they were important to my mother. She kept them. The cedar box is also full of trinkets: dried pacifiers, honor pins, a broken pink rosary, old pennies, and worn, thin-stripped, paper-handwritten, finely cut hospital infant ID bracelets wrapped in plastic. From the dates on the bracelets, I can make out which bracelet belongs to what sibling, and I count five, as I am one of four girls and one boy, the baby. In the corner there is what I thought was a black rubber ball, but once I unwrap the old sandwich bag a tight ball of black hair cushions my fingers. It is my brother's hair.

I held my brother's hair in my hand, feeling the magic and soft evidence of loving and wanting more, the best, for another human being so much and knowing that even though they came from and through you, they didn't, couldn't belong to you. At least my momma could keep my baby brother's hair. I remember that my papaw and momma had words about it.

"If you don't cut this boy's hair, I will. You got him walking around here looking like a got-damn girl," Papaw fussed at my mother.

It was the end of the summer when my brother, born in September, was one month shy of his first birthday. My mother, newly divorced with Catholic Church approval, drove six hours south from Chicago with three smaller kids to pick up me and my sister. School would be starting soon, and my mother and all my siblings would spend one week in Sparta before we made our way back north with a car full of one adult, five kids, too many cans of Shasta pop, ham and cheese sandwiches, canned green beans, collard greens, sun butter pickles, and garden-ripe cucumbers and tomatoes stuffed in Kroger grocery store bags. Papaw packed our trunk tight with so much food from his two gardens that it was a miracle that the tail of our car didn't drag the road all the way north on Highway 57.

"You know it's bad luck to cut a baby's hair before they turn one, and I'm not cutting his hair until after he's one year old," said Momma.

"Stay out of it," said my grandma.

My papaw just gave my momma a look, shook his head, and walked to the shed at the back of the house to get more canned food.

The way my papaw fussed over preparing my momma for our drive back to Chicago, I was convinced for a long time that my momma was his favorite out of all his four children, his oldest still-born. As a child I didn't understand what it was like to worry if your children had enough food to eat and that the worry never left you, however old your children became. It wasn't a wealthy White male slave owner who took Papaw's daughter north under false pretenses like Borders took Sukey: it was a city-slicker Black husband who convinced her that he would love her forever but, instead, believed marriage and gender gave him the right to treat her, a Black woman with children, like an indentured servant—a slave.

I wondered if Sukey would have kept the hair from her sons' first haircuts. Was she even allowed to cut her children's hair?

Was Sukey a *fool* to determine and act upon her and her children's worth between the seemingly continuous traveling and moving spaces and places of de facto and de jure slavery in the United States of America?

Having three children of my own, still traveling and living north like my ancestors, as my husband and our children and I live in the state known as the North Star, I cannot begin to imagine Sukey's pain, my ancestors' pain, and the pain of any parent who is separated from their child as a result of structural racial, gendered, and class oppression and violence.

However, like a descendant of an oppressed people who have experienced generational trauma, my papaw, like his sister, must have known that his job was to tell the stories, his stories, as best he could. Held captive by my childhood, my sensitivity, my respect, and my love for my elders—that is, *my foolishness*—my papaw knew that I would listen. He must have known that I was a writer, and when the time was right, I would retell those same stories, my stories, and Sukey's family story to my children and to the world.

As I sit here in Minnesota in 2023 with my beautiful fearless Black children, I write and tell them my stories knowing that we are all still moving north, simultaneously a physical and spiritual location defying time and space, trying to love and travel and move to just get and be free.

Maybe Aunt Reola understood, a Black woman descendant of African slaves in the Americas, that the ultimate freedom was the ability to tell your story, and like the Underground Railroad that carried escaped Black slaves through Sparta, Illinois, my ancestors placed and carried their stories in their DNA, in me. I became the safehouse to get them free, and like my ancestors I write my words to and for myself and my children in the hopes that they will be freer than I am.

• • •

"Reola! Leave that girl alone," my papaw hissed at her. Aunt Reola looked at me, smiled, and let me go. She waved her hand in the air at her brother for good measure.

"Bye," I said to my aunt Reola.

I used the bathroom, washed my hands, and bent down to put my mouth on the silver metal faucet and drank some water directly from the kitchen sink. Once done, I rushed back past Aunt Reola, extra careful not to step on her feet, and made my way back outside.

• • •

Later, after a supper of fried potatoes with onions, round steak, and green beans, I will ride with my papaw to return Aunt Reola to the nursing home. Once we drop her off and say our goodbyes, I will get to ride up front in the passenger seat right next to my papaw, and he will slowly take the scenic route back to my grandma's house. He will painstakingly point out the schoolhouse at the top of Eden's Hill and the burnt-red brick homes on Sparta's main street that were stations that conducted passengers north to freedom on the Underground Railroad. He will tell me general stories of slaves and indigenous peoples; he will tell me that Spirits live in the trees, so it is important to respect them; he will show me how to read the tops of tree leaves that forewarn of bad storms; and he will tell me not to be afraid when I see Spirits, because I should only fear the living and not the dead.

"The dead are not like the living. If you don't mess with them, they won't mess with you," he will say.

At the time, I will just sit in the front seat of the car not fully understanding but still hearing, absorbing, and enjoying everything that my papaw will say and show me in the soft southern Illinois generations removed from the Carolinas cadence of his voice while he drives us around. It will be many years later as an adult and after Papaw's, Aunt Reola's, and my grandma's deaths that I will match Papaw's stories and his voice's cadence with my own Chicago and Minnesota voice and stories and with the story and voice of escaped Black female mother and slave Susan "Sukey" Borders, while writing this essay.

Grown Folks' Business

On Saturdays, Momma sat alone in our yellow kitchen, smoking cigarettes and drinking Coca-Cola from its contoured glass bottle. Momma usually sat between the kitchen window and the table. Her long slender legs crossed each other, and cheap, blue flip-flops dangled from her feet. She shook one foot back and forth to the steady rhythm of the music. I sat with my sisters and brother on the couch in our sparsely decorated living room.

Our house was shaped like one big rectangle, and from the living room we watched Momma flopping her foot, smoking her cigarettes, and drinking her pop. The couch faced a big broken television set, and on top of it sat the smaller black-and-white television that worked. The room could have been improved a bit by more and newer furniture and by moving the smaller television to the bar and the broken one downstairs, but Momma wouldn't let us move the TV. It was a gift from her dead brother, Wayne.

Wayne and Momma were very close. He was the only one we saw regularly, and he brought the TV on one of his visits. He'd even shuttle us the three hundred miles from Chicago to Sparta, Illinois, and back when Momma couldn't afford to buy six Greyhound bus tickets. When Wayne died in a coal mining accident, it was the first and only time I ever saw my mother cry. She hurt so much; I wondered if she ever realized how much we were hurting, too. We tried

to convince Momma that we could carry the TV downstairs by ourselves without damaging it any further, but our suggestions, like
our questions about our parents' divorce, were always met with a
swift and solid "No."

"I am grown," was Momma's response to me and my four siblings whenever we asked her about Daddy and their divorce. Usually the question came in rare moments of play and intimacy when
Momma seemed happy and at ease. That usually meant on Saturday afternoons, when the house was clean, and everybody was tired
and a little loopy from a morning of sweeping, scrubbing, and vac-
uuming. On the good Saturdays, there was even enough food for
the weekend. Momma didn't worry about what bills not to pay in
order to pay the bills she needed to pay. Momma called it robbing
Peter to pay Paul.

Next to the television was the bar with the record player. From
black vinyl stacked on top of black vinyl, waiting its turn to drop, the
smooth seventies R&B sounds of Luther Vandross, Peabo Bryson,
and Phyllis Hyman streamed out of the record player speakers into
our small, one-story, two-bedroom house on Chicago's South Side.
Like most offspring of Motown parents, my siblings and I could
sing all the lyrics to Momma's favorite songs. It didn't matter that
we didn't understand the words, their joy, and their pain. We just
liked how happy the music seemed to make Momma feel. When we
watched and heard Momma sing those songs, she was no longer
a single mother of five kids abandoned by her husband. Momma
was the lead singer, and we were her snazzy backup singers with
synchronized moves, dancing nice and looking mighty fine in the
height of the '70s disco era.

When Phyllis Hyman sang "Somewhere in My Lifetime," I was
too young to have kissed somebody's lips in that special way that
Phyllis was crooning about, but I somehow already knew in my
heart and soul what Phyllis's longing was about. I missed Daddy,

and I missed the part of Momma that Daddy took with him when he left us. I knew that Momma missed Daddy too, and listening to music and singing together was the only time she could afford to feel it. It was during those carefree times that I, like many children of divorce, asked my desperate questions. It seemed as if one day Daddy was at home, and the next day Daddy was gone.

"Momma . . . what happened between you and Daddy? Momma . . . why isn't Daddy coming home?"

When Phyllis Hyman was playing in the background, I just knew that Momma would answer. At age ten, it was easy to be courageous. My ignorance and childhood forgetfulness made it easy to come back to the same questions over and over again. I was analytical and inquisitive, unlike my siblings. I was already a critical thinker, which in my family translated into a reputation for talking too much, asking too many questions, and having a smart-ass mouth. I was reading Stephen King and Danielle Steel novels, and I had watched too many episodes of *The Young and the Restless* and *General Hospital*. My parents even took me to see *Cooley High* in the movie theater when I was six, although I fell asleep before the good (sex and violence) parts of the movie. I thought I knew everything and that I could handle anything.

"Momma. What happened? Why is Daddy not here?" I asked again, thinking that maybe she didn't hear me.

"I'm grown," she responded for the second time.

Momma took a drag off her cigarette. Phyllis was singing "You Know How to Love Me," but right then I could no longer hear Phyllis's words or the music.

Momma stood up and placed her hands on her size-ten hips. She hung her head and turned it to the side to face the kitchen window, allowing her long, straight black hair to fall over her face. Her cigarette was gone, and she calmly reached down over the kitchen table to free another Winston from its squished red-and-white package. The sound of the match striking and lighting sucked in the room's silence.

I looked back into the living room to see my oldest sister, Cheron, sitting on the couch. She was giving me a look that said *Shut up and sit down because you are really gonna get it if you don't stop.*

I rolled my eyes at her the way good little sisters can, and I turned back to face Momma.

An exhaled white fog circled my pigtailed head like a ghost, and Momma turned from the kitchen window to face me. Her five-foot-eleven-inch frame towered over me, and through the smoke her eyes widened into my own, which were exactly like hers.

"Momma. Please tell me what happened, so I can understand?" I asked again. My desire to know was making me very brave. "Please," I begged. For some reason, her eye contact made me hopeful.

Momma's full, pink lips closed to pull in more smoke from her cigarette, and with this physical movement I knew my questions had gone too far. Our conversation was over.

I about-faced and walked back to the living room, a soldier shamed and defeated in battle. Cheron gave me a smug I-told-you-so look. A little of my pride was intact because I knew Cheron had the same questions, but she didn't have the guts to ask. Cherisse, Jacqueline, and Ronnie were too young to care. For most of their lives, Daddy had hardly been at home. It seemed that I was the only person who couldn't let it go.

In Momma's world, children did not ask adults questions. Adults were grown; therefore, adults were absolved of all self-explanation, especially to their own kids.

"It's not fair, Momma! It affects us too!" I yelled at her from the living room into the kitchen, knowing that I was cutting it really close. It was a safe distance, but even from the living room, I stepped back a little in case her hand robotically sprung out of the kitchen to slap me in the face. Momma did have magical powers.

"If you ain't paying the bills, then sit your ass down and shut up!" Momma yelled back. It was her only response, and it was Momma's motto. I believed that it came from *The Black Momma Handbook, Volume II*, which included popular Momma phrases like "I'm not your friend, I'm your Momma," "I brought you into this world, and I'll take you out," and "Have you lost your mind?" The first volume is subtitled *None of Your Business Because I'm Grown.* They were phrases that stung harder than any open-hand slap in the face, and they cut me to the bone.

Momma's smoky silence left me in the preadolescent haze of my longing, but she clearly conveyed what my ten-year-old brain and heart could not understand: she and Daddy were through, and he was never coming back home. Although it affected me in every fiber of my being, to my mother it was absolutely none of my business.

Before the divorce, I remember school mornings filled with hugs and kisses. When we left for school, Momma always licked her thumb to wipe dried breakfast cereal from the creased edges of our mouths. Late in the afternoon, we ran to the bus stop at the end of the block to greet Momma and walk her home. But when Daddy left, we, like most single-parent families, were instantly thrown into poverty; we lived one paycheck away from starvation and being homeless. Momma's communications became primarily fierce directions of survival: "Take care of your brother and sisters." "Keep the house clean." "Leave me alone, because you always want something." And "I can't never have nothing because of you!" I learned early on not to want anything or at least not to show I wanted anything, but I could never stop wanting to know why my parents divorced, and why my father left us and never came back.

• • •

According to my paternal grandmother, who prided herself on being lighter than a paper bag, Momma was having too many kids.

It didn't matter that Grandmother had five kids of her own. Grandmother could do that because she was middle class and her husband hadn't left her.

"She just kept popping them out," Grandmother said as she rubbed her chest underneath her weekend robe. It was an involuntary movement and something that seemed to soothe her. She often was relaxed and in her best moods when she was wearing her weekend robes and rubbing her breasts. It was Sunday morning, and sometimes we stayed Saturday nights and all day Sundays with Grandmother. She read the paper and watched the White Sox or Cubs on WGN if she wasn't torturing us with straightening our hair with chemicals.

As a hard head makes for a soft behind, one of our favorite topics of discussion was how sorry she was over Momma and Daddy's divorce. We were lucky to see my father once or twice a year after the divorce.

"I know it hurts, but at least you have a father," was always her response to my eternal questions of why, what was the last time she saw my father, and did she know where he was at.

"Your grandmother never knew her daddy," she said about herself, as she rubbed one breast, then the other. The rubbing seemed like a form of meditation, and I wished, at age ten, that I had breasts to rub, too. Maybe it would make me feel better while I listened to her stories.

My grandmother migrated from Arkansas to Chicago as a young girl. Her father's name was Red, and Red made a living playing piano in juke joints across the South. Grandmother's mother, Beulah, babysat Red and his wife's children when Red traveled and when his wife worked. Red came home a lot when his wife wasn't there. At the age of fourteen, Beulah gave birth to Red's fifth daughter, my grandmother, and Beulah's family quietly shipped "adopted" Grandmother to Chicago to "stay" with relatives.

Grandmother didn't see her father much. When she was a toddler and still living in rural Arkansas, Red took her to the home, the back door to be specific, of his Irish father. Apparently, Red hadn't grown up with his father either, but he wanted the opportunity to show off his beautiful, light-skinned daughter with her red hair to his white father for approval. Grandmother's family never talked about Beulah's rape, Red's pedophilia, and Grandmother's abandonment.

It seemed that fatherlessness, secrets, and abandonment were a family tradition, and Grandmother really believed that that kind of hurt was normal.

"Pain is a part of life, child," she slipped into Black vernacular to finish her point. We as children weren't ever allowed to use nonstandard English around my grandparents, or we would be slapped in the mouth.

"Why?" I asked.

"It just is, baby. Be grateful for what you have, because it could be worse," she said, and her attention went back to watching the White Sox and rubbing her breasts. Grandmother was so sincere. What was being a child of divorce compared to never knowing your birth father and birth mother?

To Grandmother, I was lucky and spoiled, and she was doing me a huge favor by encouraging me to learn to live with my parents' divorce and my father's absence. Hadn't she done a good job learning to live with her hurt? And her parents weren't even married, let alone courting. What right did I, a little Black girl from Chicago with black nappy hair, have to expect a normal family life with my father?

"After your mother had the second baby, Grandmother asked your daddy if they were using something," she said, coming back to what she thought was the most important point of our conversation. Grandmother regularly referred to herself in the third person.

"What do you mean?" I asked, really understanding but wanting her to explain.

"They just kept having children, one right after another, and Grandmother wondered if your mother had ever had the talk about birth control. You know . . . ," she said.

The White Sox hit a home run, and her attention left me and her breasts. She jumped up and ran to the television, screaming, "Yes! Yes! Yes!"

I thought that maybe my parents just really loved each other. Isn't that why they had all those children? Is it possible that my parents' love was really about lust dangerously paired with my mother's fifth-generation Roman Catholicism?

Grandmother said that she wanted somebody to talk to Momma, and I have always wondered why didn't she just talk to Momma herself. Who would talk to my mother? If these people couldn't even tell me why my parents divorced, how could they talk about sex, birth control, and babies? Everyone that Momma ever knew was more than three hundred miles away in her small, rural hometown. All of Momma's married family and friends disappeared the day she left my father.

Who could Momma trust enough to tell her to stop having children with the Black man, with much darker skin than hers that she dared to marry and that she loved, but who did not really love her? Who loved Momma enough and knew enough to tell her that?

If they did tell Momma, what did they say to her?

"Your man loves you, Cheryl, but he is no good for you, girl," or "Cheryl, you better get a hold on yourself tight so that you won't end up in a jam with all these children."

Maybe that was the mistake: thinking that the children were the jam, that the children, like spoiled leftovers, were the problem when love and a marriage ended.

No one said anything. They kept silent, and I kept asking questions.

By the time they said anything, it was too late. My siblings and I were here, and saying something about it became gossip, judgment, and talking behind my mother's back. They said nothing, and another woman, another Black woman, another poor woman, another single mother, another Catholic woman, and another inner-city woman almost choked herself to death on her own love and her best effort to take care of her children.

• • •

I have a sort of bald spot on the back of my head. It is short and smooth, like freshly trimmed grass, right at the place where my head hits the pillow when I sleep on my back. It is my habit to periodically touch it and think about it involuntarily. It is not caused by male pattern baldness or hair breakage. I was born with a full-size afro, which was appropriate to 1969. It was only when women other than my momma started putting their hands in my hair that I was made aware of the bald patch.

It was Cheron's job to braid hair in our house, because Momma didn't have time to do our hair. Plus, Momma didn't have a nappy piece of hair on her body, so she really didn't know how to comb the coarse hair of her own children. One day while Cheron was French-braiding cornrows into my hair, she crudely informed me of the spot.

"I can't braid your head here in this spot," she said as she yanked on the small patch.

"Ouch," I said. I pulled away.

"Be still, or I won't braid it," she said, and the thought of looking ugly for the next week made me put up with the pain.

On other grooming occasions, it was my next-door neighbor

and sometimes babysitter, Doll. I cringed when Doll pressed my nappy black hair in that spot with her hot comb and Blue Magic grease, because the short hairs couldn't protect my tender scalp from the fiery heat of Doll's metal comb.

"What are you doing in the back of your head, girl?" Doll said out of one side of her mouth while her cigarette hung out the other.

I stayed silent. Doll had sugar (Black vernacular for diabetes), her husband died right after he bought her their first and only house, and it was rumored that her daughter ran away from home after she beat her with a white extension cord. She watched neighborhood kids to make money on the side. Doll was seriously old-school. Doll asked children questions that were not meant to be answered. The question itself was the statement.

The patch on the back of my head needed different treatment when my grandmother first straightened my hair with lye. After she worked me over with her scalp-burning chemicals in her basement-wannabe-beauty-salon, I placed my head under her professional hairdryer. When Momma came to pick me up, Grandmother boasted proudly that her work, the destruction of my coarse hair for straighter, whiter-looking hair, was a masterpiece of orange plastic rollers, except for the smaller green ones. Grandmother motioned me to get out from under the dryer, and she pushed my head down with her hand for Momma's inspection.

"It's beautiful, Cheryl, expect for this spot in the back of her head. What happened?" Genuinely puzzled, they stared at the back of my head for a moment, and I stared at my big feet and the floor. While Momma and Grandmother tried to imagine why I had such a marking, the green magnetic rollers, my newly processed hair, and I hung on for life.

"I think I can cover it up," Grandmother broke the silence and the staring, and it meant I could go home believing I looked beautiful, at least for that day.

• • •

According to my Aunt Linda in a conversation we had after my mother's death, my father was cheating on my mother with a woman who lived in the neighborhood. My mother convinced my Uncle Harold (my father's brother and Aunt Linda's ex-husband) to take her to the woman's house. It was a hot August day in 1969. My mother found my father with another woman at that house. I was born a few weeks later.

My father was not only having an affair with the woman, but he had furnished the woman's bedroom when he and my mother were living in a house with no furniture at all. I cannot imagine how devastating that was for Momma. To have one child not even a year old, one child about to be born, to have left your family, your hometown, and your pursuit of a college education for a man, and to find he was cheating on you, your child, and your unborn child with another woman.

I imagine that after I was born I lay in the crib crying a lot. I imagine that I was never picked up. I imagine Momma not having the physical and emotional energy to do anything beyond nursing me. Because I now consider myself an emotional eater, I imagine that breastfeeding time was the only opportunity I had for love, comfort, and attention. It is in the months of crying in the crib, neglected because I could not walk like my sister, that I developed the bald patch on the back of my head.

• • •

"You were a titty baby . . . always on your momma's titties" is one of the only memories that I have of my father talking about his only memory of me as a baby.

• • •

"I should have known," Momma said.

Two plastic cups full of pop and ice sweated out a late June day on our concrete steps. Aunt Linda was visiting us on her way home from work.

Aunt Linda and Momma were very close. They had a great deal in common. They were both married and divorced from Coleman brothers. Their conversation was free flowing, and because I had finally gained a little grown-folks status, I was not asked to leave the porch to let grown folks talk their business.

I was no longer an adolescent in the kitchen singing Momma's favorite songs. The seventies were over, I was in college, and it was a Friday. It was one of those good days. There was no music playing. There were Pepsi and cigarettes, two of my mother's favorite things in the world, and there were fewer mouths to feed in the house. Three of her children were away in college, and that left only two kids at home. Plus, the Cook County courts had decided in Momma's favor, so Daddy was still paying child support, back child support, and health insurance for my youngest sibling, my baby brother.

Now, let's be clear. There was no way I was ever going to be grown enough to smoke cigarettes or try to drink Momma's Pepsi out of her cup, but I could stay on the porch and listen to her talk if I played my cards right. I had to be cool, and from the way I liked to ask questions, you all know that cool was a very hard thing for me to do.

Aunt Linda and Momma were talking about Momma's first meeting with Daddy. They were riding a bus in Carbondale. Daddy said that Momma had the prettiest legs he had ever seen, and Momma said that Daddy was a little young but smart and handsome. She said when Daddy smiled it was like the slow opening of a dark house to morning sunlight.

"I should have known," she said again and took a long drag off her Winston Light 100s.

"Should have known what?" I asked. I was trying to be really cool.

"This is grown folks' business, Taiyon," Aunt Linda said. She stood up from the concrete porch and faced Momma from the bottom of the steps. They both laughed.

I was losing my cool.

"I should have known then," Momma said. It was becoming a mantra, but finally the story came, and I got the business.

Momma had a serious collection of Motown forty-fives when she met Daddy, and their relationship started with them just getting together to listen to her music. Once they were a hot and heavy item, Momma said they were planning to attend a big campus dance together, but Daddy said that he was sick and didn't feel like going. Momma initially decided to stay home with her girlfriends, but later she and her girlfriends went to the party anyway. Momma said she found my father at the dance hanging out with another girl. She said she tried to confront Daddy, but he just ran away.

"It was like that the entire time we were married. He was with me and everybody else, too, but this time I didn't have anywhere to run. I just should have known," she said for the last time, and it sounded like the words meant something different to her because they meant something new and different to me. It was as if I heard the words and their meanings for the first time.

"I told you it was grown folks' business," Aunt Linda said, and she laughed, knowing Momma's story had not satisfied me as she watched me look at Momma. Aunt Linda shrugged her shoulders, took a drag off her cigarette, and drank the remaining Pepsi from her cup.

I suddenly felt shy and looked away from Momma's face. I should have known, too. I should have trusted Momma to have a really good reason. I should have trusted Momma to be grown.

• • •

Unlike me, Momma was cool.

Momma said the important things just once, and if you didn't listen, the consequences were all on you. This was her way. She never pushed me into anything I didn't want to do. She would always make a suggestion, and she would leave the decisions up to me, even when she saw me heading for an obvious wreck. I guess she knew that wrecks cannot be stopped, at least not by people standing on the sidelines.

"How old is he?" is the only question she asked me. We were talking on the phone about the trouble in my marriage. My first husband could sell sand in the desert, and it did not help that he believed that he was God's sexual gift to every willing woman who crossed his path.

"He is thirty-two years old," I replied. There was silence on the line, and then Momma spoke.

"He is not going to change. He is going to be that way forever, Taiyon." She said it calmly without any hint of persuasion. It was a fact offered to me without any judgment or chastisement. It was a fact given to be left or taken.

"It's going to hurt," I said, trying not to cry. I didn't want to show myself as weak to Momma. I was embarrassed and ashamed enough that I had married a complete idiot, someone even worse than my father. But I was lucky. I had finished college, we had no children, and we owned absolutely nothing together. It would be a divorce free of legal problems and, most important, the scars would only be internal. My price for failure would be permanent but manageable unto myself. My price would not be as high as Momma's.

"It's going to hurt," I said again, pretending that Momma didn't hear me the first time. I wanted her to give me a way out, but this time she came back with a quick response.

"Yes, Taiyon, it will hurt, but you'll live," she added the words like forgotten items on a grocery store list. Oh, I almost forgot. I need the tomatoes and onions to make the stew, and the pain and the hurt is an integral ingredient of life, especially when mistakes, change, and the hope for something better are involved.

Momma was giving me the best advice she could give. I knew that it was as persuasive as she would get. She knew love was blind, and she would never try to convince me to do something that I was not ready to do. It was advice she had learned the hard way. I would be a fool not to listen.

By this time, I still knew only a little of why Momma divorced my father, and why it took her so long to leave him, but the small details were no longer important. The big things—commitment, responsibility, love, trust, and self-respect—were.

At twenty-six, I could finally start to see my mother as not just my mother but as a brave woman who risked everything. She swallowed her fear, her pain, and the abandonment and judgment of others because she knew there must be a better way to live a life than allowing herself to be continually hurt and humiliated by another person, even when that person was her husband and the father of her five children. In that moment of talking about my divorce with my mother, I became grown. I was thankful Momma left Daddy. Who might I have become had she not?

• • •

"I just got the papers today. The divorce is final," I said over the phone. It was around nine in the evening, and it had been almost five months since I filed. I had just arrived home from a seminar in my first year of graduate school to find my final documents. Without thinking, I immediately called Momma to give her the news. I wanted her to be proud of me.

"Good. It is done," she said, and it was a short conversation. We said "I love you" to each other, and I said I would call her the coming weekend. It was our last conversation. Before the week was done, my mother went into cardiac arrest and never regained consciousness. It happened at home in the kitchen. For the first time in twenty-six years, Momma was alone in the house. My brother, the last born, had left for college earlier that year. There was no one at home to call the police, to unlock the bolted doors from the inside, and to revive Momma's heart in time. By the time the paramedics did arrive after breaking into the house, she was revived, but her brain had gone too long without oxygen. As she had wanted, we removed Momma from life support and let her go.

• • •

Momma went to the grave at age forty-nine, never telling me the entire story of how and why she and Daddy divorced. I guess for so long Momma was forced to focus on survival that she didn't talk or share about how she felt. Her job was just to make sure that the five of us had food, shelter, clothing, and a decent education. The basic necessities of life didn't include the privilege of emotional well-being or putting all your business in the street. Momma worked full time, and fulfilling her parental responsibilities sucked away everything else, including her ability to share the pain that all of us were going through. For a long time I even thought that she didn't love Daddy and that she didn't really love us. For a long time I thought that she didn't love me. But she did love me. She was only a Black woman, with five kids, trying to be grown.

Poems as a Mapping of Human Potential

An oral ruttier is a long poem containing navigational instructions which sailors learned by heart and recited from memory. The poem contained the routes and ties, the stars and maybe the taste and flavour of the waters, the coolness, the saltiness; all for finding one's way at sea. Perhaps, too, the reflection and texture of the sea bed, also the sight of birds, the direction of their flight. This and an instrument called a Kamal which measured the altitude of stars from the horizon.

—Dionne Brand, *A Map to the Door of No Return:*
Notes to Belonging

When I first read Lucille Clifton's "for the bird who flew against our window one morning and broke his natural neck," I couldn't believe that she could put that bird into a poem: first alive and then dead. As a Black girl growing up within the internal and external effects of institutional, historical, and structural racism, sexism, and poverty, I had grown used to hearing voices that were not my own and being left to shape myself out of the skins of others. Clifton's *good woman: poems and a memoir 1969–1980* was the first time I had read poetry, heard voices and narratives that intersected the first person, families, death, pain, love, gender, race, poverty, beauty, oppression, and more, which seemed to convey identities and experiences to which I could connect. Clifton's recurring images and metaphors of birds, flight, and death in the collection were like a legend that unlocked and revealed a map of birds, narratives, emotions, and epiphanies from my own human experiences.

As a map of personal and/or universal narratives, images, and emotions that can disrupt linear time and point of view, a poem uses language and space to navigate and record epiphanies of human identity and experience, which in turn creates a map of human potential for the possibility of compassion, empathy, and understanding for its readers. Poems as maps unlock human potential because the reader has the possibility through reading and interpreting a poem to discover, recognize, and comprehend identities and experiences that are applicable to self, applicable to others, and applicable to the larger world. In this vein, the interpretation of the poem as a map is subject to infinite and mutable interpretations and applications.

I was twenty-seven when my forty-nine-year-old mother died suddenly. After the funeral, my youngest sister told me about a dream she had right before our mother's premature passing. My sister said that she was alone inside our childhood home on the South Side of Chicago, and there was a black bird flying around in the living room, trying desperately to get out of the house. She said that every time the black bird hit the wall and hit the ceiling, a great burst of bright light, like a supernova, would appear from the bird's impact points, and then my sister said that she just woke up.

I don't know if she remembered the bird from auntie's house when we were just little girls. When I was a young girl spending the summer in a small town directly east of the Missouri Mason–Dixon line in southern Illinois, my sister, my cousin, and I found a brown baby bird lying in the grass on the side of my cousin's house. It wasn't dead; it just couldn't fly, so it made perfect sense to us to put the bird in a shoebox. Somehow we knew not to touch the bird with our bare hands, and we placed the baby bird in the box with some green leaves and dried twigs. With well-made plans to play "healing veterinarian" with the bird the very next day during our play, we hid the shoebox in my cousin's bedroom closet for safe-keeping. We might have even pilfered a juicy pink earthworm from my uncle's styrofoam bait bucket for good measure.

The feathered patient forgotten, we went on with our summer day of hanging upside-down on the broken swing set, sucking on sour rose-colored crabapples that fell to the ground, and playing hide-'n'-seek in the creek. My aunt fried fish for dinner, and we ate white Wonder bread, meatless spaghetti, cold coleslaw, and catfish with red hot sauce at the round kitchen table until it was hard to breathe. After being teased by my coal-mining uncle for our constant kid bickering, we brushed our tiny teeth, bathed our prepubescent bodies, and were still small enough to sleep three in my cousin's rainbow lace canopy bed. The next morning we woke to the baby bird tweeting, peeping, and streaking in and out of my cousin's bedroom while my auntie, dressed in her sheer green nightgown, ran around the bedroom and the rest of the house waving the yellow kitchen broom in the air like a mad witch doctor, failing miserably to catch the zooming resurrected bird.

"These goddamn girls have brought a got-damned bird into my house!" my auntie screamed and cried while she beat the broom against the bedroom walls and through the window curtains with one hand and held a Kroger paper bag in the other. My sister, cousin, and I just sat up in the bed too afraid to move and our heads dizzy from trying to track the swift bird with our human eyes. Eventually, Auntie got the bird out of the house, and I had never seen Auntie, my mother's younger sister, so afraid and so mad even when her husband called her a fat-assed heifer for taking too long to bring him beer from the icebox. As we prepared for our obligatory beating with a switch from the weeping willow in the yard, we could hear Auntie still fussing back and forth with Uncle about the bird. My cousin, my sister, and I had violated, and clearly the switch was punishment for bringing the bird into the house, even with the best of intentions. While the long, thin, green stick smacked, whizzed, and popped across the chubby caramel flesh of our exposed legs, Auntie repeatedly told us like a rosary chant, in time with her whips, to never, ever be stupid girls that bring fowl into the house because having a bird inside the house was a sure sign of impending death for someone living in that house.

Now I am not necessarily saying that I believe that birds inside one's house is an omen of human death; however, I can write that my auntie emphatically believed this to be true. Knowing that this was what my auntie believed helped me to locate an actual place and space for not only how my auntie understood and experienced birds but also how she lived and perceived her life. I gained insight, compassion, and respect for her reverence for nature and a higher power, her respect for things that she did not understand, her fierce protection of and devotion to her family, the acceptance of her own mortality and the tragic irony of the human life, and the almost overwhelming beauty of her sheer strength and will to survive and thrive despite the challenges. Auntie's location on a map orient me on my own map, as my story (position) was/is connected, a measurable distance relative to hers.

Auntie helped raise me, she loved me, she fed me, she clothed me, and I, like her children, witnessed and experienced parts of her life that became parts of my life, too. A beautiful young Brown woman with two children, Auntie had not always been sad, morbidly obese, battling "sugar," mean, and verbally abused daily by her husband and sole provider. Unfolding her map and plotting its points with respect, compassion, and empathy revealed a passage into my auntie's life and world, different but no less real than mine. I got it. For what is a trapped bird in her house but a reminder of how she too was once flying free and high in the open sky, and through the promise of love from a bow-legged Black boy who carried a high school football all the way into her heart, Auntie became confined within the domestic intersections of the constructed identities of gender, race, place, and class weighted down by larger and cumulative historical and institutional structures. Birds were once dinosaurs.

A poem as a map, if successful, crosses boundaries of identities and experiences that allow readers to build roads and bridges across the unknown borders that often keep us from each other and from our own humanity. The poem as a map has human potential, which allows readers to witness and coordinate individual identities and experiences within larger cultural, historical, and social contexts. This layering and placement of personal and universal, or internal and external, allow a witnessing, a recording, and a talking back that gives forth human agency and hope. Out of Clifton's poems I was able to gain an insight into my own experiences and voices that helped me to create my own poems of maps of understanding, which deepened my humanity, respect, and understanding for my experiences and the experiences of my family.

From the map that Lucille Clifton provided me through her words, lines, and stanzas, like a cartographer I wrote several poems about the individual death of a young single mother within the structural context of generational poverty, segregated housing, and racism on the South Side of Chicago; I wrote about the spiritual and physiological injustice of long-term systemic poverty on the individual Black female body through the larger lens of urban pollution and low-quality health care for poor women of color; I wrote about catfish and domestic abuse in the context of southern Illinois coal miners losing shifts and a small town printing plant closing to move jobs overseas; I wrote about the Chicago gun violence that threatened my little brother with a bullet that barely missed him but tagged his friend and how that bullet is directly connected to the shooting of Trayvon Martin; I wrote about the grief and tragedy of unforeseen loss of my mother's Black body in the context of U.S. racial disparities, police violence, and the national value of Brown and Black lives; and I wrote about a pretty middle-aged superstitious Black woman who doesn't like birds in her house, has a white great-grandmother, and lives down the street from the town country club that still doesn't allow nonwhite members more than twenty years after desegregation. I have used my poem maps of compassion, empathy, and respect for my auntie's and my mother's stories so that the poems become more than just objectified stories. Their poems as maps utilize their voices, their images, their emotions, and their experiences of their internal and external lives to pinpoint a space and a place of meaning and significance that otherwise could not be located on a map whose dominant topography has been historically exclusionary.

Sometimes the poems as maps can become counter or relief maps of resistance through identifying tangible and nontangible impediments of the human journey that are easy to miss because of historical and cumulative systems, institutions, and constructed maps, particularly for marginalized bodies, to create better outcomes or at least outcomes that can be understood and subsequently charted and mapped. Poems as maps have the human potential to affect change and transform. The poems as maps can replace outdated and silencing maps and narratives. These locations, like map triangulation, document and record the subject(s)' existence, their humanity, their value and work to create infinite meanings from which we, as readers, can learn and be transformed. Poems as maps answer the questions, "How will I make it out of this, how can we change this, what happened, how did this happen, what else was happening when this happened, who did it happen to, how can I understand it, why does it matter, and how is it aesthetically beautiful and valuable?" Poems as maps help readers make sense of and survey self and experience. As you read, survey, locate, and orient your position relative to poems you encounter, consider the words of J. Drew Lanham:

> unfurl the map
> aim the camps well
> cause true north does lie
> dead reckon instead on reality
> find yourself there

Poems as maps chart an event or a series of events played in a time of the poem that contours and collapses the distance of knowing between the poem and its reader. In this way, like the bird in Auntie's house that navigated me to a greater world of understanding, action, and expression, I am hoping that poetry as a map just might reveal a path or grid that will allow us to locate one another and save us from ourselves.

Disparate Impacts

Moving to Minnesota to Live Just Enough for the City

In 1998, I was accepted with full financial funding into two pres-tigious graduate creative writing programs: one at a university in the Deep South, and the other at a university in the North. I already knew that the artist Prince (my music boyfriend) lived in Minneapolis, Minnesota, so I decided to visit the city of Tuscaloosa, Alabama, in order to make my choice. What little I knew of the southern United States came from the *Eyes on the Prize* documentaries and the Hollywood movie *Mississippi Burning*.[1] As a native of Chicago, Illinois, I had lived almost the first two decades of my life on the city's South Side, always geographically above the Mason-Dixon Line. Somewhere near the Ides of March, I set off

---

1. Like any good Catholic Black schoolgirl raised in the United States during the 1970s and 1980s with middle-class values without middle-class money, what I learned about drugs, sex, alcohol, and racism was through *ABC Afterschool Specials* and dramatic documentaries about slavery and racism of the southern United States. See the film *Eyes on the Prize: American's Civil Rights Years 1954–1965* (1987). I saw *Mississippi Burning* with my first boyfriend, my first love, who was also a Black nerd: chemistry major. At the time, we were both poor and first-generation college students raised on the South Side of Chicago. We're still poor. After watching this movie, we made a serious pact that we would never live below the Mason-Dixon Line. Eventually, I discovered that he cheated on me, we broke up, and when my mother died almost ten years later, he sent me a condolence card postmarked from Orlando, Florida. Traitor!

on my tourist-and-idealist drive to southern Alabama. I blasted Chicago house music on the speakers of my red Hertz rental, and I drove alone from Sparta, Illinois, through the Mississippi River Valley heading south, with the explicit and repeated directions from my maternal grandparents to make sure that the car's gas tank was completely full and my bladder completely empty before I arrived at the Popeye Bridge.

The Popeye Bridge (so named to honor the creator of the cartoon character Popeye the Sailor Man, E. C. Segar, who was born in Chester, Illinois) crosses over the Mississippi River from the bluffs of Chester, Illinois, into the southwest part of Missouri, the Show Me State. My maternal grandparents, who were born, raised, and came of age in southern Illinois (the Land of Lincoln) during the Great Depression, were not much afraid of escaped inmates from the Menard Correctional Center (formerly known as the Southern Illinois Penitentiary), which is located in Chester and home to notorious, diabolical, and insane criminals such as American serial killer John Wayne Gacy. An entertainer by trade, Gacy "became known as the 'Killer Clown' because he lured his young unsuspecting victims into his home before killing them," and he buried the bodies within the concrete, walls, and crawl spaces of his home.[2] My grandparents were more afraid of the historical, ongoing, and de facto legacy of Jim Crow physical violence. They extracted yet another promise from me not to stop my car for gas or a bag of spicy pig skins (fried pork rinds taste better in the South), or to take a bathroom break at all in that part of Missouri until I (directly inside my car) passed the state line into Arkansas, all before dark. And I set off.

---

2. U.S. American serial killer and sexual predator suspected of killing up to twenty-nine men and boys and burying the remains of the bodies within his Chicago-area suburban home. His neighbors complained of a distinct "smell" coming from his property, which led to his arrest. Gacy was executed by lethal injection in 1994. See Aamer Madhani, "Indiana Killings a Reminder of John Wayne Gacy," *USA Today*, October 21, 2014.

From the time I crossed the Popeye Bridge into Missouri, my grandparents had me all hyped up, looking for Ku Klux Klan members randomly popping out of the southern shadows at me, from the back seat of my rental car. I passed through the Missouri city of Cape Girardeau[3] and made my way to Arkansas (the Natural State), where I stopped for gas and to use the bathroom. (I stopped compulsively glancing in my rearview mirror every twenty minutes once I left Missouri.) From Arkansas, I drove through Tennessee (America at Its Best and/or Agriculture and Commerce), Mississippi (By Valor and Arms), and finally into Alabama (We Dare Defend Our Rights). I was a northern Yankee hot mess—a Black woman from the North in the Deep South for the first time, jacked up on cultural and historical knowledge from mass-produced liberal media primarily made of dominant and mainstream historical narratives and images of U.S. racism and waiting for something bad to happen.

As I drove along the outskirts of Birmingham, I knew the city was connected to important U.S. history such as the civil rights movement and the Birmingham bombings,[4] but ironically, I just imagined how, from my car windows in the month of March, Birmingham looked like any other American city from a red rental car speeding down and speeding south from the north on a federal highway. No one said, "Lookie here, girl" from the back seat of my rental car; no one tried to lynch me when I gassed up my car; no

---

3. Birthplace of Republican and conservative media icon Rush Limbaugh. I thought this fact might be useful in building tragic irony and satire in this essay. In the summer of 2000, when I traveled I-35 North in Iowa to teach speech communication at a local community college, I listened to Limbaugh on conservative talk radio, and I would laugh my ass off for the entire thirty-minute drive. There was no greater high! Man, I still remember that—that shit was really funny. I would hit the steering wheel of the car with my hand, never imagining that what Limbaugh was saying could ever really become mainstream. Guess who's laughing now?

4. In 1963, there was a church bombing at the Sixteenth Street Baptist Church that killed four African American girls. See Spike Lee's 1997 documentary 4 Little Girls.

one tried to burn me on a cross when I used the toilet; and no one spit in my food and/or beverage (scene from *Roots*) when I bought my meals from the fast food drive-up windows. (Or at least I believe they didn't spit in my food; I guess I can't vouch for this one, as pop/soda is carbonated and can easily conceal spit bubbles.)

In less than twenty-four hours, I had made a solitary drive crossing five southern states in a red rental car from Hertz; the trip was really the plot for a bad but predictable misogynistic movie about a serial killer that preys on single young females. Okay, I am not a White female, but close.

For the most part, by this time in my trip I queued the house music to my internal soundtrack and I thought to myself that attending school and living in southern Alabama for three years was actually possible. It was the turn of the century, wasn't it, and wasn't there a chance that I could be the Black Flannery O'Connor?[5] I was fifth-generation Roman Catholic on my mom's side, and the Black stuff could be easily worked out. (I now am a first-generation Recovering Catholic from over five generations in America; I don't know what kind of Catholics my maternal line was before.) Just details. Right? What was this *Eyes on the Prize* stuff about, anyway? If I extracted the occasional jolting southern accent heard in passing through a rural gas station or from a fastidious and polite worker at a fast food drive-through window, people and their southern cities, through my eyes during this trip, seemed pretty much the same as cities and people in the urban North. (It is important to note here that I am sure my city-slicker, fast-talking Chicago accent was equally as jolting to southern ears as well.) By the time I made it to the outskirts of Tuscaloosa and to the university, I was convinced that my grandparents had totally hyped me up for no reason.

---

5. One of my favorite writers after Zora Neale Hurston, Toni Morrison, Alice Walker, and Nikky Finney.

In southern Alabama, the flowers were in bloom, and the city was like a beautiful woman, my beautiful woman. After seeing her and smelling her for myself for the first time, how could any writer from the North, visiting the South for the first time, fail to make such a cheesy, sexist, and gender-constructing analogy for the beauty of the southern U.S. landscape in the spring? I was an urban northern city girl, and I saw colors and flowers that I didn't even know existed in nature. Some of the flowers were so huge to my urban concrete eyes that it was like they were from the 1976 movie *Food of the Gods*, without the gigantic killer rats.[6] I made my way to my motel, for which the university graciously paid. By the morning after my breakfast of bacon (real pig meat), biscuits, sausage (another type of real pig meat), eggs, syrup, and sweet iced tea (with no spit, guaranteed, I might add), I was sold on the southern life, hook, line, and sinker![7]

Once on campus, I made my way to the department's graduate writing program, and I was greeted there by warm and sincere (White) faculty members.[8] I thought that they were all really nice and thoughtful. There was one designated Black Female Graduate Student (BFGS) to show me around. BFGS and I left the department to tour a little of the campus and to take a look around the city. I queued up my house music soundtrack on my internal twelve-inch vinyl record player, and the BFGS and I were on our way. In our enthusiasm, we were a little like Dorothy and Toto from *The Wiz*, happily headed off to the Emerald City, once they had been assuredly pointed in the right direction.[9]

---

6. Again, '70s and '80s television, while safe but not equitable, provided most of the cultural and folklore education for me and my sisters when we were not allowed to go outside.
7. I am currently working on an essay titled "Paula Deen, a Baked Potato, and Compassion."
8. To my knowledge, there were no tenured Black instructors at that time in their graduate creative writing program.
9. I need to stop here, lest we become caught up in which one of us was the dog, me or the BFGS. It's *The Wiz* instead of *The Wizard of Oz*; it's in Harlem, not in Kansas, and I am

The first time that the needle scratched clear across the twelve-inch vinyl was when I spotted the Confederate flag. Time stood still. I imagined that I must have passed countless Confederate flags on my drive from Illinois to Alabama, but for some reason, standing with the BFGS, this was the first time I had noticed it. I wondered if my perception of the South had changed because my physical position in the South was different: I was no longer a single solitary Black person.

When I stood with the BFGS, she and I had formed a group. We had become more than one Black person within a physical space historically and contemporarily dominated by a structure of White male patriarchy, which depended on the historical invisibility, blindness, and silence of our Black and Brown bodies in order to continue to thrive and survive. Like a flat balloon inflated by air, together the BFGS and I helped each other take shape and form. Our Black bodies became visible within a space where we seemed not to exist before. This new visible space (our changed spaces) of multiplicity, visibility (being able to be seen), and our vision shifted our power as Black women and our power as Black people in that time and space. It triggered the ability for us to (seemingly) magically appear and to magically see, too, what we (I for the first time) hadn't consciously seen or recognized before: the big-ass Hollywood *Gone with the Wind* Romantic movie version of Confederate flags all over the freaking city.

My acknowledgment of seeing the Confederate flag in the physical presence of another Black body shifted our dimensional positions, our visibility, and ultimately it shifted my vision. I saw what I

---

in Alabama; it's Motown, Berry Gordy, Diana Ross; Diana means Goddess of the Hunt; somebody had an affair with somebody in power; this person did a gangster move, and then this person stole a movie part from a young blood (at the time); and see . . . but by that time, we lose focus. This analogy might not work. Wasn't Glinda the Good Witch of the South? That's deep, y'all.

had not allowed myself to see before. This city, what I once thought of as an attractive pretty lady, kind of like Glinda the Good Witch, was no longer a woman I wanted to be around, let alone love. The flag's visual presence worked to threaten us, to put us in our place lest we became too powerful, and all too clearly it conveyed the social, political, and racial ideology of the region, despite its luscious and decadent "womanly" spring welcome. I guess it was even worse, since we (the BFGS and I) were supposedly educated (learn-ed) and free Negros: insert Frederick Douglass here.[10] I wondered if the BFGS ever noticed the Confederate flags when she was just alone in Tuscaloosa by herself. Maybe BFGS had been desensitized, caught up in her ongoing solitary singleness. She was the only Black student in the program at the time. I looked at my new BFF, the BFGS.

"Are those Confederate flags everywhere?" I asked her.

"Yes," she said.

"Oohhh . . . kaayyy," I said very slowly, and then I asked her what, judging by the look on her face, must have been the most stupid question on Earth: "Don't the Confederate flags bother you?" My eyes got really Diana Ross big, as I looked at the BFGS, searching for some sign of camaraderie.

"It's the South," said BFGS. The BFGS just shrugged her shoulders and seemed slightly annoyed with me. I guess I was ruining her Dirty South soundtrack and the party by pointing this symbolic shit out to her. (No disrespect intended.)

I thought to myself that maybe I was overreacting; you know we Negros from the North have been rumored to be historically problematic. So we walked to her car. BFGS preceded to show me, like a Black Vanna White, the sights of the campus and the surrounding

---

10. In Douglass's slave narrative, he notes that the first time he fully understood his oppression was when he learned to read, which further underscores why it was illegal to teach slaves to read and write. Slaves who have the capacity to fully see, comprehend, and communicate the structures of their own oppression were/are dangerous.

neighborhoods of the university town where many students lived. The happy feelings from our first meeting in the morning had now faded, as I now saw the Confederate flags everywhere. I couldn't stop and not see them if I wanted to. Confederate flags on cars, Confederate flags waving on tall poles in front of residential and public buildings, Confederate flags on T-shirts, Confederate flags on pens and pencils, Confederate flag diapers, Confederate flags on condoms, Confederate flag tampons and maxipads, Confederate flag bandanas, Confederate flag Band-Aids, Confederate flag earrings, Confederate flag wallets, Confederate flag underwear, and Confederate flags taped to car windows, bumpers, and license plates. I even found a brand of hot and spicy pig skins in a convenience store with Confederate flag packaging. My internal house music soundtrack wasn't coming back. I was tripping, because no one was really freaking out about the Confederate flags, including the BFGS. I became jumpy, expecting a noose and a mob of folks covered in white sheets with guns to jump out at us at any moment. Clearly, I was the only one with the problem and most likely the one to be killed if we were jumped by a deadly race mob—or at least I would be the first one killed, and killed slowly at that.

"Some folks I hang out with from the university are having a get-together this evening. Do you wanna go?" the BFGS asked and simultaneously changed the subject. She too could sense that the energy had shifted between us.

"At night?" I asked her. I don't know who has eyes bigger than Diana Ross, but this time my eyes were bigger than Diana Ross's.

BFGS just looked at me and flared her nostrils. I almost thought I could hear her saying something about Black Yankees. She was so done with me.

I pumped myself up with an internal pep talk, as the twelve-inch vinyl to my theme song was completely scratched by now, and I just kept chanting to myself over and over again that it's just a flag. It's just a flag. It's just a flag. It's just a flag. It's just a flag. There's no place like home. There's no place like home. There's no place like home.

Once we looked at BFGS's apartment as our final stop on the city tour, we made our way to eat lunch, which was at a popular seafood restaurant chain, and my soundtrack was back in full force, as nothing takes my mind away from pain and trauma like food.

After lunch, the BFGS drove me back to campus. She was nice, but clearly our time was over. Looking back on it, I realized that in my explicit acknowledgment of the Confederate flag, I had revealed myself as a certain type of Black person, and my presence in the BFGS's sphere of identity production and existence in southern Alabama was not welcomed. I was a bad (not in a good assimilated way) Negro! The Confederate flags and the actual historical and structural racism that they explicitly celebrated and represented were not the problem. No, *I* had become the one that made it hard for the BFGS to exist and hide inside the solitary crawl spaces of White structural supremacy in Alabama. I wanted to say to her, "Dude. You are the one who is actually trapped inside the wall and not me. I'm free."

But instead, I was the disruption that scratched BFGS's needle across her twelve-inch vinyl record. I guess that if I wasn't with BFGS, the Confederate flags in Alabama did not have to exist, and with a bad Black person like me there, she would be in danger of becoming a certain type of Black person to herself and in the eyes of others.[11] With me not there, BFGS could be anything but a BFGS who was a descendant of African slaves, living and learning in

11. Not bad Negro or bad Black like *Spies of Mississippi* bad; those were some really badly constructed bad Negroes recently revealed from under the cover of darkness (pun intended). More like Black Lives Matter bad. It's the deconstructed Negroes who are the worst! See the 2014 documentary *Spies of Mississippi: The Campaign to Stop Freedom Summer's Civil Rights Movement of 1964*.

a university town wholly and presently constructed as a result of cumulative historical and institutional structures immersed in the celebration of White supremacy and its histrionic historical narratives and symbols inside and outside of the university. Inside and outside of her, it seemed to pin her down, and I wondered whether she could feel it breaking through her skin.

I, my red rental car, and my judgment all made our way back to the motel for the night. The next morning, I left the university and its town for my northern drive back to Illinois. As I left town, I knew that I would not attend the university. In my naivete, I had thought before my visit that I could be comfortable with such explicit and conspicuous symbolic displays of White supremacy. As a result, I thought I had better options.

• • •

Shortly after I received my acceptance to a creative writing program for a university in the state of Minnesota (Land of Ten Thousand Lakes), a program instructor called me at home to personally persuade me to attend their program. Our discussion was warm, welcoming, and inviting, and ultimately, I was flattered, honored, and excited about the wonderful possibilities of learning, creativity, and experience that I was going to learn, create, and have. After my spring break trip to Alabama, I thought that Minnesota was far enough north, and it was the home to my music man, Prince, so of course it definitely could not be as racist as Alabama. Right? I decided to attend the writing program in Minnesota.

Although my paternal granddaddy, Frank Coleman Sr., was born in Mississippi in the 1920s, it would be years before Granddaddy would begin the ritualistic regurgitating of his young man memories and retell stories of his forced departure from Mississippi, which bodily purged him at the age of fifteen under an immediate threat of a night lynching. In moving north from Mississippi, my granddaddy was following his mother and his younger brother, by way of the city of St. Louis, to the South Side of Chicago as part of his Great Migration.[12] Little did I know that when I decided to attend a university in Minnesota that I would be continuing that migration north and west. As Stevie Wonder put it, we were "living just enough for the city."[13] Although I was nervous, I was extremely excited to finally be making my dreams as a writer come true in a place that I assumed was safe. By the time I had settled into Minnesota, I saw no conspicuous displays of Confederate flags.

All incoming students to the writing program were required, as a cohort, to take a seminar taught by one of the established faculty members. As first-year students, we shared brief manuscripts in our genre with the seminar faculty and our cohort classmates in a workshop over the duration of the semester. The seminar classroom was intimate and small, and all the students fit snugly around the table while the instructor sat at the head of the table. The instructor discussed our various manuscripts, one by one, in front of the entire class. As new students, we had this opportunity to introduce ourselves and our creative work to our program cohort, peers, and future career colleagues.

"Tai, I read your manuscript, and there are numerous errors, and I think you need to take some grammar classes," the instructor said to me during class one afternoon, in front of all the students.[14]

---

12. See Isabel Wilkerson, *The Warmth of Other Suns: The Epic Story of America's Great Migration* (New York: Vintage, 2010).

13. After raising five kids alone on the South Side of Chicago, my mother lost consciousness while talking on the yellow kitchen phone to her secret boyfriend in 1997. Eight months earlier, she watched me graduate from college, the first of her children and the first one in our family, on both sides, to do so. I walked across the stage in Ames, Iowa, and once I arrived on the other side of the stage, my momma greeted me and kissed me full on my lips like I was a little baby. By February, she was on life support. It would be Stevie Wonder, my mother's music, who got me through and helped me make sense of hard times, with both joy and pain, when she was no longer physically there to set me straight.

14. I have the name Tai because when I first moved to Iowa to attend college, no one could

Some of my classmates snickered, and some of them just looked away, never making eye contact again with me for the entire semester, and some never made any eye contact with me for the remainder of the entire program.

"The characters in the poem are Black and urban, and they are using Black vernacular. They are from the inner city of Chicago. I am from the inner city of Chicago, and I write from some of my personal experiences and voices. This is one of the reasons I decided to attend a creative writing program, because I thought there was space to write like this creatively," I said back to the distinguished faculty, politely and proudly, without even thinking.

By the time I had started their graduate writing program, I had already completed a master's degree in English and had been teaching college-level composition for more than two years in the United States and abroad. I wondered if the instructor had read my application, my application manuscript, and my student profile. I wondered if the instructor's statements were tied to the easiest point of reference for someone who showed up looking like me: Black, first-generation university student on both sides of my family, fat, urban, working-class, and female. I guess I didn't look like the typical Minnesotan, nor did I look like the typical graduate student relative to the program's dominant student demographics. I definitely didn't look like the instructor; nor did I look like anyone in the seminar room.

"Well, you won't get published, then," the instructor said to me in a matter-of-fact tone that quickly quieted the room. The instructor's, the program's, and the institution's ethos in that moment depended on them being right and depended on my subsequent

---

pronounce Taiyon, so they, my new White college friends, gave me the nickname Tai and it stuck. So if someone today calls me Taiyon, they either really know me (know me and are related to me by blood or Chicago friendship); they are really serious; or I'm in trouble. See Toby versus Kunta Kinte in *Roots*.

demise as a writer and as a Black woman writer. All my classmates, who had been out drinking with me the night before, quickly looked away again.

There was no discussion of the content of my work: the themes, the characters, the style, and its legacy, position, and discourse within the canon of similar literary works and authors. In that moment, a constructed institutional stereotype had been tied around my Black neck like a loose rope with the threat of its threads tightening the more I resisted. If I stood my ground, the noose would only continue to constrict. If I gave in and assimilated, there might be hope for me, my work, and my neck. But then, in that moment with the criticism and stabbing words of that instructor, I was now just the racially constructed and undeserving Black Female Graduate Student (BFGS) granted admission to a competitive graduate program because of affirmative action policies. I wanted the carpeted floor to swallow me up, but I thought of my strong Black single mother instead.

• • •

I am the second oldest of five kids raised by a single mother. From the time I turned fifteen, I always had a job, in order to help my mother out. When I was in high school, I worked at a McDonald's in a western suburb near Chicago, which often required me to ride a bus one hour each way. At least once a week, I had to be part of the closing team, and I would leave work at one in the morning on the bus. That one-hour bus ride became a cumulative two-hour trip home: a bus ride to the 95th and King Drive Station, a bus ride to 103rd Street, and a twenty-to-thirty-minute walk home because the bus didn't run past my house at that time in the morning. Even with the illegal mace and stun gun that I always carried, it was a dangerous journey, but I had no choice if we wanted to eat, and if I wanted new clothes and underwear. During those times, my mother taught me to always look people directly in the eye whenever I was alone and walking in public, especially at night.

"If you think that they might try to steal from you or rape you, don't look away, *Taiyon*," she would say to me with a cigarette in one hand and a cup of coffee in the other. "Let them know that if they come after you, that you gonna fight them hard, and they will decide that you are not worth the trouble and leave you alone." Sharply these words would leave her mouth, and then she would take a drag off her Winston cigarette and exhale smoke up in the air.

"Do you hear me talking to you, girl?" Momma would ask again, in response to my silence, to make sure that I heard her.

"Yes, Momma. I hear you," I would respectfully respond.

• • •

The memory leaves, and I am back in the intimate seminar room in the state of Minnesota with my esteemed instructor, but it feels like the corner of 103rd and Michigan Avenue on Chicago's South Side outside the liquor store and White Castle at two in the morning. I am walking fast and looking in all directions, one look after the other, to be prepared for an attack, but it is really the turn of the century, I am in Minneapolis, and the leaves outside the seminar graduate classroom are turning into fall. The instructor is looking at me and waiting for my response.

"Well, then . . . that's not a place where I want my writing to be published," I said, without even batting an eyelash, while I dropped the microphone. A collective gasp could be heard throughout the room. My mother, who by this time had been dead for over a year, would have been proud.

It is only later, when I am taking the bus home from the university and walking from Nicollet Avenue to my apartment in South Minneapolis, that I feel the body pains that had grown into wounds from the instructor's well-intentioned words. It would be the first of many institutional scrimmages, microabrasions, and microaggressions that would plague my experiences as the only BFGS and writer within a predominantly White university writing program—a program that had generously funded my participation, a program that had attracted me and persuaded me to attend. But what I found and experienced instead within the university's walls was canonized book lists from majority core program courses taught by some instructors that failed to include any writers of color; being told by some faculty that any graduate student creative writing about race, ethnicity, and sexual orientation as subject and theme was "pat" and that race had already been done before, and it was exhausted, so please do write about new subjects and themes; some instructors advising me that *I* was racist if I wrote about race, and they sometimes forbade the topic of race for seminar papers and presentations; being advised by some instructors not to expect favors, because clearly that is the only way I, as a BFGS, made my way through academia; never seeming to have the opportunity, as my White student program cohorts did, to develop sincere mentoring relationships with some instructors because they saw me and my work as something they could not or did not want to connect and/or relate to; being advised by some instructors that it was inappropriate to talk about and to question the lack of equity in the program among instructors, curriculum, pedagogy, and students during program meetings where instructors had specifically asked for feedback from students regarding their experiences in the program; some instructors only discussing my writing in terms of sentence-level constructions and never in terms of its content and themes; and being told by some faculty that I should just focus on the mothering and raising of my recently born baby as opposed to advising me regarding next important professional options and

steps upon the completion of a graduate degree in writing.[15] However, the university willingly used my body's photographic images
in its periodicals and publications and productions to demonstrate
the welcoming environment and equity of its university and program.[16] Even the cheery photos, as sometimes I was placed with
other Brown and Black marginalized bodies, didn't quite reveal
how my body was painfully contorted to fit inside program spaces.

During my time attending the university, my Black body was
meant to be embedded and hidden inside the walls, the crawl
spaces, and the concrete of the university's institutional structures.
My Black female body was not meant to be seen, to be acknowledged, to be heard, or to be discovered anywhere in my creative
work or within the program itself. Eventually, through my experiences, I discovered facts that I would only tragically realize later
should have been of significance to my research selection process
when choosing schools and places to live. In 2014, an online journal article ranked the state of Minnesota as the second-worst state

15. In a required graduate seminar, I proposed writing a paper arguing that Mary Shelly's
Frankenstein was the literary construction of the nineteenth-century Enlightenment
"nigger" in the text. The instructor denied my proposal, telling me that there had been a
recent shooting and subsequent death of a White person that took place in a local neighborhood frequented by graduate students at the university. The suspected shooter was
Black. The instructor told me that my paper topic and content would upset the White
graduate students who had been affected by the shooting; thus the instructor would not
approve my paper topic and content. The instructor advised me that I was being racist
and insensitive and asked me the question, with clear, physically shown frustration, "Why
does it always have to be about race?" With compassion for any loss of life, I am still trying
to figure out what the shooting incident had to do with me and my graduate work. The
only thread that seemed to connect it was that I was Black and the shooter was Black. The
instructor, the graduate student, the murder victim, and Mary Shelley are/were White.
Frankenstein wasn't White.
16. Negro Teflon Deflector Shields (NTDS) Up! My colleague and I, both Black women
who teach at predominantly White institutions, joke that some educational institutions
use strategically placed marketing images of their Black, Brown, and other marginalized
bodied members as deflectors, an obscuring agent, against any critiques (internal and
community), discourse, and changes regarding equity.

for Blacks to live, in the areas of home ownership, incarceration, education, and unemployment. Alabama did not even make it into the list's top ten.[17]

Unfortunately, these institutional experiences and impersonal policy and procedural points of institutional and structural inequity happen to all graduate students regardless of their identity positions and intersections within their respective institutions, but these daily microaggressions and microabrasions are disproportionately more damaging to marginalized bodies because of the legacy of our historical and institutional positions. Minnesota is now home to me and my family, and we have had great experiences here for which we fully recognize, are fully grateful, and fully value. There were supportive instructors, I have a great job (knock on wood), I exist and intersect within amazing diverse and dynamic communities, and my family and I experience our own intersections of privilege. But there has to be a place to voice the challenging experiences too, in hopes of learning, creativity, and improving the experiences of others.

When I left my apartment that morning before the writing seminar, I was happy, the air was crisp, and the sun was bright in a blue sky free of clouds. From what I had assumed that day when I first woke up and looked out my apartment window, the weather would be warm. As a result, I wore a light jacket instead of something heavier. By the time I arrived at school, I was freezing my ass off, and I explained this to the department secretaries and janitors I had befriended, as they were much nicer and more welcoming than my classmates and some instructors. It seems that those of us who don't belong can easily recognize each other, and unlike the other BFGS, they didn't throw me under the bus. After my story of

---

17. Thomas C. Frohlich et al., "The Worst States for Black Americans," *24/7 Wall St.*, December 2, 2014. http://247wallst.com/special-report/2014/12/09/the-worst-states-for -black-americans/.

freezing cold in what was to be my first Minnesota winter, they all laughed at me and advised me that the coldest days in Minnesota are when the skies are the clearest pretty blue, amazingly sunny, and completely and beautifully free of clouds. They laughed at my ignorance in not preparing myself for the onslaught of the obvious cold weather. There was no bridge for me to cross, no state lines, and/or multicolored flags to indicate that territories and ideologies had changed.

After enough microabrasions, I longed for the Confederate flags of the South, because at least the South had clear lines of demarcation and warning. In Minnesota, there were only smiling faces, open classroom doors, and a stinging persistent coldness that let me know that I was in a new, different place that wasn't really welcoming—and that this place was resistant to me calling it home. Later that evening, I crossed the Mississippi River on my way back to my apartment, and by the time I got to the building, I had to pee so badly that I had trouble unlocking the door. I made it just in time. As I sat on my toilet stool in absolute safety, I thought of the other BFGS—not the BFGS that I too had become—and I wondered, Would she ever have attended a writing program in the North instead of a university in southern Alabama, if she had had the choice? Maybe she knew what I failed to realize during our short time together: there are Confederate flags everywhere, even in places where we can't see them.

The Dangers of Teaching Writing While Black

"*Nigger* is just a word."

Those five words were my piercing introduction to being an African American female teacher and graduate student in the field of composition pedagogy. Even now, more than two decades later, those five words remain a dominant memory of my experience earning my graduate degree in English.

It was a composition pedagogy and curriculum course for first-year graduate students, and I was a proud and excited member of the cohort. We had received teaching assistantships as part of our graduate school funding package, and we were being trained to teach college-level writing.[1] The class was being team-taught by

---

1. As the first person in my family to graduate from college, I was not only geeked that I had been accepted to graduate school. I really didn't discover teaching composition as a career until my first year of graduate school. Initially, it seemed like it was just a big secret to people like me who have institutionally, historically, and cumulatively not had the opportunities to pursue advanced education and the resulting career opportunities. So, dude. I was, like, I could actually get *paid* for reading and writing and then teaching reading and writing to people, and I could wear blue jeans and Birkenstocks to work and that was an actual career? I was already doing that, and I would totally do that for free. It is and was fun! Dude! For real for real—two times unbelievable! When I was awarded an assistantship in graduate school to teach freshman composition, I felt like I had won the lottery and had been admitted to a secret club. I was, like, where do they do that at? To me, it was like the *Saturday Night Live* "White Like Me" episode (1994).

two instructors, one *constructed* as White female and the other *constructed* as White male.

At the time, the terminal degree offered by the university was in rhetoric and professional communication (RPC), and the RPC faculty theoretically managed the composition program, including training the new graduate teaching instructors. The class was pedagogically structured around the theoretical belief that all writing is an argument and around Aristotle's methods of persuasion. Readings about the art of constructing arguments, studying famous persuasive arguments, and class discussions were the primary content of the course. Toward the end of the course, students were tasked with developing writing course syllabi, writing assignments, assessment tools, and a theoretical and methodological rational narrative as support for our pedagogical delivery of the freshman composition curriculum.

$$\bullet \ \bullet \ \bullet$$

"What did you say?" I responded back to the professor.[2] I was sure that I had misheard her.

I was never allowed to use that word.

I didn't use that word, and I couldn't understand why she was using this word in our classroom. I tried to look into the faces of my fellow students and future professional colleagues for help and support while the professor looked at mine, but my fellow students looked away.

The class was working in small groups, and the professor pivoted and turned in the middle of the room to ensure that she made

---

2. There is a reason that it has taken me more than twenty years to finally be able to look back in an attempt to write about and understand this experience for the purpose of utilizing this experience as a way of decolonizing the composition classroom to improve my teaching, to continually interrogate my own positionality, and to improve the experiences of my students.

eye contact with everyone. I looked at the members of my small group, which just happened to be all the constructed people of color and other marginalized folks in the room: two African Americans (including me), one Afro-Latinx, one White LGBTQ+ female, and one Muslim student. The remaining and dominant number of students in the classroom were constructed as White American.[3]

"*Nigger* is just a word," the White female professor said for the second time. She was short,[4] and I swore that she bounced slightly up on the balls of her feet in beat, two times, with the consonant sounds in the word, *nig-ger*.[5]

We had read many essays and books, including *Pedagogy of the Oppressed* by Paulo Freire and the classic "Just Walk On By: Black Men in Public Space" by Brent Staples. Freire's text links the struggle of oppression to understanding one's position to the world and power central to the educational process and, in my view, to writing (literacy) acquisition. Staples writes about how his education did not prevent him from being viewed through gendered and racial stereotypes. There was discussion of words and their constructed meanings, and the professors emphasized how *all* words only have

---

3. Beverly Daniel Tatum, *Why Are All the Black Kids Sitting Together in the Cafeteria? And Other Conversations about Race*, 5th ed. (New York: Basic Books, 2003).

4. I am still amazed that short is a recessive gene and that there is a bias toward tall people and power in the United States. During a hiring committee training at work, I was amazed to learn that people have an implicit bias toward people who they perceive as tall. We were given statistics that most CEOs, U.S. presidents, and other powerful people, primarily men, were or are over six feet tall. This totally amazed me as I am six feet tall, and I have had a hard time accessing power as a tall, fat, African American female. In addition, in my house everybody was so tall that the kids in the neighborhood called our house the Valley of the Giants, but what kind of power did we have?

5. Yes. She said this word in the actual classroom, and she was not referring to the country in Africa. See U.S. Ambassador Joseph Wilson IV's op-ed "Debunking Distortions about My Trip to Niger," *New York Times*, August 17, 2004.

power when people who use and hear those words are complicit in the construction of the power: blah, blah, blah, and super-blah.[6]

So I asked a person in the classroom, who is a descendant of African slaves in the United States, if he was only offended by the use of the word *nigger* because he was complicit in creating its derogatory meaning at the moment the professor let the word *nigger* slip from her lips. It seemed that I just had to merely concede that in the professor's use of the word *nigger*, she wasn't really acknowledging the racist, violent, and hegemonic social historical, political, and exclusionary affect and effect of the word on me as an African American and others as non–African Americans in the classroom. It was just a word. Right?

Wow!

It was like magic!

Where had this theory been all my life, especially when I had been subjected to equally derogatory argumentative identity words of bitch, hoe, slut, darkie, dumb, lazy, stupid, fat, and pussy, to name a few? I was trying really hard to understand how our class lecture arrived at this vast breach in the classroom knowledge and experience. I was also trying really hard to ignore her, but I am not really good at that, so I went back into the conversation.

"Excuse me. I am sorry, but I didn't understand what you said." I thought that was a good place to start.

I looked the professor directly in her eyes, and she showed no signs of retreating. I was new to graduate school and the ways scholars boldly manipulate and use theory to obscure and perpetuate the silence and invisibility of the Other and their experiences. The other groups stopped working, and the class fell silent. The male professor made his way over to our group and positioned

---

6. It is what Jacques Derrida calls a "detour" from the text. See Derrida, "Difference," in his *Margins of Philosophy*, trans. Alan Bass. (Chicago: University of Chicago Press, 1984).

himself closer to the female professor. The male professor didn't repeat what his colleague said, but his physical proximity to the professor's body was a show of support, and his colleague went back in for the kill.

"*Nigger* is just a word. Rhetoric is a form of communication, and words only carry the meanings that we give to them," she explained like she was explaining how to solve a variable equation on the board for the third time. In that moment the professor created a paradigm where our identities and experiences of meaning could not exist simultaneously. My identity and experiences had to die in order for hers to dominate the classroom discourse, her lesson plans, and meanings that she was so well-meaningly creating for the classroom.

Cue lovely jazz elevator background music.

• • •

A year before that class, I was a senior English major in the fall semester of my last academic year completing graduate school applications and making career decisions. I had nobly rejected the pristine law school application that my very supportive and sincere academic adviser tried to pass to me three times[7] while sitting across from her in her small office.

Like some first-generation Black folks one to two generations geographically removed from the U.S. South, I grew up in a segregated northern inner city in the seventies and eighties. It was a place and time where if you could string a well-enunciated sentence together and all your verbs conjugated correctly with the help of *Schoolhouse Rock*'s "Verb: That's What's Happening" on Saturday mornings, everybody said that you were "articulate or well-spoken"

---

7. "Truly I tell you," Jesus answered, "this very night, before the rooster crows, you will disown me three times" (Matthew 26:34).

and that you should go to school to become a lawyer.[8] So growing up and throughout the majority of my undergraduate career, attending law school after graduation was my plan. No shade to lawyers, but if believing in the study and practice of law as my career path (along with believing that it would allow me to one day buy a blue Mercedes for my momma because we never had a car and blue was my momma's favorite color) got[9] me out of the South Side of Chicago to become the first person in my family to complete a college degree, then Patricia J. Williams and Johnnie Cochran was where it was at.

I couldn't really tell anyone that I wanted to be a writer. After undergraduate years of studying English Literature and student activism, I was sincerely convinced that I didn't want to work in a professional field where I could so compassionately empathize why, in some social situations, citizens were set up to break laws and subsequently be subject to inequitable outcomes. I could have never imagined that a year later I would be in a graduate composition pedagogy class with a White professor using racial epithets with Montresor's impunity as a methodology for teaching me—a first-generation African American female student—a lesson on

---

8. My father would actually pop me and my siblings in the mouth if we used words like *ain't*, or *dere* or *dis* instead of *there* and *this*. My grandfather (who migrated at age fifteen to Chicago from Mississippi and never graduated from high school and is the smartest man I know) would even pretend to not hear me speaking to him if he believed that I asked a question in a manner that was not spoken well. See Lynette Clementson, "The Racial Politics of Speaking Well," *New York Times*, February 4, 2007.

9. My granddaddy would object to the use of the word *got*, the past tense and past participle of *get*. (See Webster's definition.) My composition teachers always told me that formal writing does not quote the dictionary because it means that one didn't do any *real* research. In my literature and composition classes, I tell my students that *got* is an informal word choice and/or language and that the word should not be used in formal, academic writing. I tell my earnest and well-meaning students to find a synonym like the verb *have*. The word *got* is sometimes the only word and the best word and verb to use. Didn't somebody say that in good writing there are no synonyms?

argument.[10] And I thought teaching writing would be a safe space for me as a woman of color.

• • •

In that moment, the teacher called me a nigger and did it legitimately because it was within her academic freedom and purview. Because rhetorically *nigger* is just a word. Right? Poverty, homelessness, oppression, learning differences, class differences, and incarceration are just things. Right? Sexual assault, homophobia, bullying, and disabilities are just things. Right? Students are just bodies that we, as teachers, have the power to mold and to control how we want without really seeing who and what they are and the myriad of ways that they may show up.

Maybe this is what happens when we teach in spaces, and we don't acknowledge and humble our pedagogy and curriculum to the world in which we and our students inhabit. Those worlds can be the same, simultaneous, overlapping, intersecting, or completely isolated.

The sad part is that I think that the professor, like many of us who teach, sincerely believed that what she said and did caused absolutely no harm, so I don't write this essay to shame or blame. I write this essay to release myself and others from the trauma experienced in the writing classroom, and maybe through compassion and empathy my experience can heal and inform our field and us (practitioners, teachers) as we work to transform in the changing dynamics of higher education with a focus on social justice, diversity, equity, inclusion, and antiracism to better teach and serve our students and intersecting community members.

---

10. See Edgar Allan Poe's story "The Cask of Amontillado."

• • •

In working toward action and solutions in our composition pedagogy, consider the following questions:

- How is my *nigger* experience as a student like the community college composition classroom when we as teachers may teach as if we know more about our students than the students know about themselves?

- How is my *nigger* experience as a student like the community college composition classroom when we as teachers may teach as if we know more about ourselves than the students know about us?

- How is my *nigger* experience as a student like the community college composition classroom when the class pedagogy and curriculum may be framed from dominant perspectives?

- Who *gets* to speak in our classrooms?

- Who *gets* to tell their stories in our classrooms?

- Who *gets* to interpret what those stories and words mean?

- Whose meanings and languages are privileged in our classrooms?

- Who and what are really dominant and centered in our classrooms?

- How might we, as well-meaning and well-intentioned teachers of community college composition, do similar damage in the classroom when we as instructors fail to humble ourselves to our own privilege and the

finite ways in which we can reentrench disparities
through our pedagogy and curriculum without even
realizing it?

It is a problem that faces the field of composition in the community
college classroom, but it is also a problem that I believe faces the
United States. We must admit that the community college composition classroom at a micro level can reflect the historical, cultural,
social, and political dynamics and legacies of power and oppression
relative to identities at the macro level, which are embodied, consciously and even more subconsciously.

• • •

In 2002, I started my first full-time teaching job at a community
college in Brooklyn Park, Minnesota. My primary courses were
college composition, developmental writing, and literature. After
two years of teaching, I was tenured in the system. In one English
composition course, I had many students who identified as Liberian refugees from the Liberian civil war.

Brooklyn Park is a suburban city north of Minneapolis and
home to the largest Liberian population in the United States. After
the first week of the course, which involved introductions and getting to know one another, my Liberian students gifted me (with
some snickering and laughing) a large poster with the names and
pictures of all the Liberian presidents, starting with the first president, J. J. Roberts, listed in chronological order. I thanked the students for their generosity and thoughtfulness, and I told them that I
would hang the poster in my office, which I proudly did. The snickering and the laughter only increased, because the students realized that I did not understand the significance of their gift.

I got it, but I didn't get it.

One kind male student came up to me in front of the class and

slowly placed his finger on the poster right on the name of the thir-
teenth president of Liberia, William David Coleman (1896–1900).
According to the poster, Coleman was an Americo-Liberian originally from Kentucky and was known to have had a strong interest in education while he was president. The student removed his
finger from the image of Coleman on the poster and pointed it directly at me. The entire room broke into laughter, and we smiled
and laughed together, trying not to cry. As we laughed, I did not
tell them about number twenty on the poster's list, William Richard Tolbert Jr. (1971–1980), who has my paternal grandmother's
maiden name of Tolbert.

Like many U.S. Americans at the start of the twenty-first century, I knew very little if anything about the Liberian civil wars
and the history of freed African American slaves in Liberia from
the nineteenth century, but I took what I thought I knew and developed a lesson plan for the diagnostic writing assignment for our
composition course. This assignment is a short writing response to
an arbitrary prompt, which allows the instructor to assess students'
writing at the start of the course as a baseline for the course's pedagogy and curriculum.

Believing that the students (their identities, voices, and experiences) should be the center of the composition classroom, I showed
the PBS documentary *Liberia: America's Stepchild* as the prompt for
the diagnostic assignment. At the time I thought, What could be
more relevant to the experiences of my students who were predominantly Liberian refugees? I was so ecstatic and proud of myself because I believed that I was providing my students with an interesting
and relevant text as part of my inclusive pedagogy and curriculum.

Halfway through the showing of the documentary, two young
Liberian male students started talking loudly. Their loud and fast
talking turned into yelling, standing, and finally pushing. I stopped
the documentary and turned on the classroom lights. Many students

were sitting at their desks with tears rolling down their faces. An older Liberian male student (the same student who had generously pointed out Coleman's name on the poster and who I would later learn had been an army medic during the civil war) separated the two fighting students. All the students spoke amongst each other in Liberian English admonishing, soothing, and eventually establishing quiet and peace in the classroom, and still I didn't understand.[11]

The two fighting students calmed down and took their seats. The older Liberian student who had stopped the fighting apologized to me on behalf of all the students in front of the class for their behavior. He explained to me that the two students were from opposing sides during the Liberian war, and unfortunately, they hadn't yet healed and that "their war" (his words) had continued on in the Liberian community as they adjusted to coming to America from the refugee camps.

• • •

"What country in Africa are you from?"

I lost count of how many students (Black and White, rich and poor, new citizen and old citizen) asked me this question during my first year teaching composition at the community college in Brooklyn Park.

"I'mfromtheSouthSideofChicago!" I would let the words roll together out of my mouth in my best South Side Black vernacular with incredulity.

I had something to prove. Couldn't my students see that I was a Black, African American, poor, and first-generation college student just like them? Life and college, like for many of my students, had not been a straight and easy line for me. (It still isn't.) I dropped

---

11. Michaeleen Doucleff, "From 'Big Jues' to 'Tay-Tay Water': A Quick Guide to Liberian English," *National Public Radio*, November 7, 2014.

out of school and graduated with an associate of arts degree from a community college before completing my undergraduate degree after a five-year hiatus.

When I started teaching at the community college, I believed that I had street cred because not only had I struggled to complete my education, but being a student in college composition courses and writing had never been a cakewalk for me.[12] I believed that I was just like my students, so when my students' first identity assumptions about me as a teacher were that I was not like them, my feelings were really hurt. I would go home and complain to my East African husband, and he would only laugh and tell me that I couldn't see myself as they saw me.

$$\cdots$$

By showing the PBS documentary that day in class, I wanted to see myself and the students through the limited and biased framework of my constructed identity paradigms: national, political, historical, racial, gender, sexual orientation, class, education, language, living in peace versus war, privilege, etc. My understanding of their identities as students in the composition classroom was only relative to who I believed I was within my constructed identities. It was as if it didn't matter that I was aware of the Americo-Liberian experience and how it oppressed indigenous Liberian people and how that experience ultimately contributed to the Liberian civil wars and to the subsequent violence, trauma, and displacement that eventually led to my students being in my composition classroom in a community college in Brooklyn Park, Minnesota.

That was wrong; I was wrong.

---

12. Gandhi Lakshmi, "The Extraordinary Story of Why a 'Cakewalk' Wasn't Always Easy," *National Public Radio*, December 23, 2013.

• • •

As community college composition instructors we do have a choice as to whether or not we recognize it.

As an educated African American and American with privilege and with the paternal surname Coleman, I was something different and something more to my community college students than what I thought I was, what I could control, and what I could actually see myself. My life intentions, my training, my profession, and my position as instructor did not matter when it came to not knowing what I didn't know and the very real impediment that lack of knowing can become to the teaching and learning of college-level writing in the community college classroom, especially when that blindness relates to our constructed identities that we inherit through no fault of our own and that are out of our personal control.

It was and is Sophocles-level hubris.

Like Tiresias advising Oedipus that he in fact was the cause of all the strife to the city and people of Thebes, I had to take responsibility for how my Liberian students responded in the classroom that day after watching the documentary. Unknowingly, my composition pedagogy and curriculum that day had attempted to render my students (their experiences and identities, i.e., how they see and move in the world) invisible, and they possibly reinscribed trauma and triggered posttraumatic stress episodes for my students—not to mention the damage I could have done to the integral trust and respect mutually needed for student success in the teaching of college-level writing. The insistence of my pedagogy and curriculum without prior consideration (regardless of intention) as to how it may affect my students' experiences and identities in the composition classroom was an attempt at creating a hierarchy of meaning and controlling the students' identities and experiences through a lens other than their own.

How could my graduate school professor say to me in her composition pedagogy class that "*nigger* is just a word" and never admit that she was wrong and apologize? Didn't she know and respect that I am an African American female, a first-generation student two generations removed from the former Confederate state of Mississippi, that I am a descendant of African slaves in the Americas, and my family, my people, and I have been subject to the repeated derogatory use of the word *nigger* as an explicit, pervasive, epistemological, and cumulative tool of physical, psychological, and institutional violence, oppression, and exclusion against African Americans for more than four hundred years in the United States of America? Being free, literate, and sitting in her graduate composition pedagogy classroom in the last decade of the twentieth century didn't change that.

By generously presenting me with a poster of the Americo-Liberian presidents and seeing the name Coleman as one of them, my Liberian students were generously teaching me a part of my and their history as an American that they fully knew that I didn't know.[13] The Liberian refugee students sitting in my classroom and not in Liberia, not in a civil war, and not in a refugee camp didn't change their identities and experiences just because they were now getting educated. They still looked at me and they saw an identity and structural connection to Americo-Liberians as it related and relates to their very real and ongoing experiences of slavery, oppression, violence, war, xenophobia, nativism, and displacement.

What is the pedagogical cost of domination, being right, or having complete control of "all meanings" in the composition

---

13. That was a lot of work and heavy lifting that my students should not have had to do; however, I am forever grateful. It has given me a critical framework by which to constantly challenge my positionality, pedagogy, and curriculum in real time. Change is necessary and constant in the teaching of college-level writing, especially in community college, where social justice and equity are a must!

classroom? Perhaps the dominant composition rules of reading, writing, and assessment at the college level (as a function of education) beget other modes of dominance and the subsequent classroom and institutional silence, violence, oppression, and ultimately exclusion that can/may follow?

As an instructor of a composition classroom, for me not to structurally and institutionally see myself as the students may see me is to not fully see and acknowledge the students.

How can we teach those whom we choose to willfully not see?

What intellectual and emotional cost must a composition instructor incur as to who we think we are within a historical, cultural, national, institutional, and/or structural framework in order to view ourselves as our students may see us?

In that moment with *Liberia: America's Stepchild*, I had a choice. Either plough forward with my pedagogy and curriculum and the way I see my identity as a teacher in the community college composition classroom, or respect and acknowledge the identities, experiences, and worlds of my Liberian students (human beings) and work (it's a practice) to refocus and recenter the composition classroom pedagogy and curriculum to their paradigms of identities, experiences, and meanings.

"I am sorry. Please forgive me. I didn't know," I repeatedly said to my students (Liberian refugee and others).

In our composition classroom, we spent the rest of the class period and two more class days having free-flowing conversations about their experiences during the civil war, in refugee camps, coming to America, and living in Minnesota. Outside the class, I independently worked to read as much as I could about the history of Americo-Liberians and the Liberian civil wars. Eventually, we ended up scrapping the diagnostic assignment altogether. My students wrote personal essays with secondary sources about their civil war experiences. At times it was not nice, neat, or pretty, but my students were seen and heard. More important, the students felt seen and heard, and validated students are better writers. My students, their identities, and experiences had become the center of the community college composition classroom, and although there was not scripted pedagogy or curriculum, it produced the best student writing and transformative experiences of my teaching career thus far. I learned that as a teacher I am always learning, and my teaching involves me and the students teaching one another. It is a community classroom after all.

• • •

Literacy, thinking, and writing critically, all things taught in composition classrooms, are foundational to civic engagement, citizenship, and liberalism (pursuit of happiness—self-actualization within a democracy). In this vein, our composition classrooms are the baseline and lifeline for critiquing equity and the experience of accessing the full benefits of citizenship, and they represent the hope, availability, and access to liberty and social justice for our students and ourselves. Considering the statistics around quality of life and success in the United States relative to education, it is not an exaggeration to conclude that an inability to read and write critically can lead to what Orlando Patterson calls social death if not physical death, as one's ability to read and write critically affects all facets of a person's quality of life.[14]

Looking back, I can now say that what my well-meaning professor said in my graduate composition pedagogy class was an act of racial and composition violence that produced, perpetuated, and reinscribed shock, silence, and oppression. In that moment my goal, like many marginalized students in dominant White spaces,

---

14. Orlando Patterson, *Slavery and Social Death: A Comparative Study.* 2nd ed. Cambridge, Mass.: Harvard University Press, 2018.

was just to try to stay afloat and to live long enough to remain in the class. In an inequitable composition classroom, marginalized students must survive what Melissa Harris-Perry in her book *Sister Citizen* calls a crooked room:

> Field dependence studies show how individuals locate the upright space. In one study, subjects were placed in a crooked chair in a crooked room and then asked to align themselves vertically. Some perceived themselves as straight only in relation to their surroundings. To the researchers' surprise, some people could be tilted by as much as 35 degrees and report that they were perfectly straight, simply because they were aligned with images that were equally titled.

When your body is in flight-or-fight mode, there isn't much time or physical and mental (intellectual) resources for mental sparring and defense, especially when the person (in this case the professor/teacher) and/or institution that you may have to face-off with controls every aspect of the paradigm: the venue, the rules, its assessments, and all the weapons (the language and its meanings). As a student in a college composition classroom with a marginalized identity, if you dare push back, so often the tools by which one can push back are the very tools that are equally as foreign, as Jacqueline Royster noted almost thirty years ago.[15] It is easy to spin intellectual circles around bodies that are at risk and in crisis if those very bodies are just doing their best to maintain their social and political upright position in a world that makes those very marginalized bodies feel like they are trying to stand up to no avail inside a crooked room, a classroom where a student's identity, experiences,

---

15. Jacqueline Jones Royster, "When the First Voice You Hear Is Not Your Own," *College Composition and Communication* 47, no. 1 (February 1996): 29–40.

and voices are made crooked and subservient, under the weight of dominant others and dominant constructions of meaning.[16]

• • •

In an attempt at compassion, I can't speak for my graduate instructor's intent in selecting that word as the vehicle for teaching words and meanings in argument that day. After more than twenty years of teaching composition as a rhetorical argument at the college and university level, I imagined that it was a well-meaning and well-intentioned attempt to not only introduce us to argument as a methodology in writing and writing instruction, but it was an attempt to argue (prove) that argument (writing) itself as a form or methodology could be objectively viewed, dissected, and critiqued by us—writing-teachers-in-training—without the acknowledgment and subsequent impact of participating individuals' (read: students' and their professors, in my case, White professors) historical, social, and instructional identities and experiences inside the classroom. Or maybe, the presence of non-White bodies in the classroom inadvertently restricted the language availability for use in the classroom, and the professor wanted to prove that her pedagogy and curriculum, i.e., the words she used (spoke) in the classroom, didn't need to change. In this way, intentional or not, the professor's use of the word *nigger* was a clear assertion of her power, her authority, and her hierarchy of meaning and control over me, over my body, over my experiences, over my identity, and over my academic and social future—all inside the cultural and academic fiefdom of her classroom pedagogy and curriculum.

That's a lot of power.

---

16. Melissa Harris-Perry, "Crooked Room," in *Sister Citizen: Shame, Stereotypes, and Black Women in America* (New Haven, Conn.: Yale University Press, 2011), 28–50.

The class continued, and the instructor held fast that she had done nothing wrong and that she was not offensive in her use of the word *nigger.* In her words, I was "merely too sensitive, had overreacted, and misunderstood her words and actions."

I completed my graduate degree in English writing and went on to teach composition and write—all the while working on my sensitivity and overreaction to inequity in the classroom and within the larger institution.

It has been more than twenty years since I had that experience in her classroom, and I am so relieved and grateful that I can finally stop carrying the burden of her hurtful word around.

That shit was heavy.

Here.

I have sat that word *nigger* down, and I have given it back to her, as it was all hers to begin with.

Tilted Uterus

When Jesus Is Your Baby Daddy

. . . .
'Bacca money
So we thought to do better by ourselves
To begin our next row
We would go and get him
Because he was medically degreed in baby bringing
Because he was young and white and handsome
And because of that
Had been neighbor to more knowledge
Than us way back behind
The country's proud and inferior lines . . . .

—Nikky Finney, "The Afterbirth, 1931"

It was the summer of 2000, and my pregnancy was considered high-risk because my OB-GYN diagnosed me with uterine fibroids. I woke from a deep sleep feeling period-like cramps in my stomach and my mattress shaking. I slept that night with my head at the foot of my single bed, which both my well-mannered grandmother and superstitious grandma would not have liked. Grandma always said that you should never sleep with your feet closer to your bedroom door than your head. She said it was very rude to let the bottoms of your feet be the first thing that greeted Spirits if you were so lucky to be graced with a visit from the dead during the night. Sleeping with my head at the foot of my bed was the only position where my pregnant body could feel the muggy August Iowa air being pulled into the hot and humid basement apartment by my cheap Walmart window fan.

At almost twenty weeks pregnant, the smell of everything made me disgustingly sick. It seemed that I could smell and taste someone eating a banana from a mile away. My boyfriend with Jesus's name, Emmanuel, was working a night shift at Krispy Kreme and wouldn't be home until well after midnight. When Emmanuel came home from work, I regularly made him take off his uniform and shower before he was allowed to enter our bedroom. He and his work clothes reeked so bad that I was convinced that he was just getting paid for mixing and frying sugar and shit, glazing it, and selling it as doughnuts. That night, I thought the bed moving was him, but when I sniffed and didn't detect the DEFCON odor, I knew he wasn't home yet and that I was alone. I assumed that the mattress shaking was nothing and happily closed my eyes into more funk-free sleep.

The bed shook again, and I looked to my right toward the bedroom door. My eyes opened to a pair of knees covered in chocolate-brown slacks. Don't ask me how I knew that the person was black skinned, had masculine energy, and wore a really nice eighties' television sitcom–style cable-knit sweater with patterned hues of beige, chestnut, and cocoa brown that matched his neatly pleated slacks. I didn't look up to see his face, but I intuitively knew that he was pointing over me toward the green wall behind me. I turned away from the pointing man to my left and faced the plain wall and saw nothing but rotating shadows and streetlights reflecting from the window fan, but I did hear a baby crying. The crying seemed to stop as soon as it started, and I was wide awake. Immediately, I turned back to my right, and the man standing at the foot of my bed was gone—just like that.

I wasn't new to visitors from the other side. I grew up in a family where feeling, seeing, and talking to Spirits was an everyday thing. My grandma said it came from being born with a veil over your face. Although we were practicing Catholics, five generations removed from Germany on my momma's side, talking with the dead beyond Mary and Jesus wasn't really viewed as double-timing Christ, especially if talking to the dead brought much needed "tea" from the other side: dreams of slithering snakes to let you know to watch out because someone you really trusted was going to betray you; regular warnings to ignore short and dark haints (ghosts) promising winning lottery numbers and other secret riches in exchange for your soul. My grandma's best girlfriend, who died young, regularly entered the world of the living through my grandma's south bedroom wall to forewarn Grandma first of her son's death and then later of her daughter's, my momma's, death. Uncle Freddie, my grandma's dead brother, who died in a car twisted around a sneaky bend on a southern Illinois back highway after too much whiskey, always confirmed Grandma's suspicions of Pawpaw's infidelity with that light-skinned hussy at the bar. And the old white lady, the former owner of my grandmother's nineteenth-century home, stomped nightly through the shotgun hallways and seemed to really get off on revealing herself, only her head, in full living color to folks who were courageous enough to sleep in her former bedroom and make the fatal error of looking up at the ceiling right before they fell asleep.

"Did you know who it was?" Grandma would ask me if I saw or sensed somebody when we spent our preteen summers with her.

"No," I responded.

"Well. They ain't gonna bother you if you don't bother them.

Don't be scared. If you are scared, just ask them, 'What in the name of the Lord do you want?' and they should go away. It is the living that should scare you and not the dead," she always calmly replied.

• • •

About two years earlier, in 1998, I had lost a baby at six weeks. I had no pain or other symptoms, except for some spotting. If it weren't for a faint blue line on the Walgreens pregnancy test and the absence of a regular period, I wouldn't have known any difference in my body. In some ways, it was like it had never happened. I had just finished graduate school, and at the end of the summer I realized that I had missed my period. I went to the doctor's office. My sister and I were the only Black people in the waiting room of the clinic, and we seemed to wait forever. Finally, a nurse called me to the front desk of the clinic and asked me to go pee in a cup. I followed the nurse to the back, entered the bathroom, peed in the plastic cup after wiping from front to back with a moist towelette, and followed the nurse back into the public waiting room. The nurse told me and my sister to remain in the public waiting room for the test results. My sister and I kept looking at each other, wondering if we stunk or something, because we wondered why the nurse, a White woman, couldn't just allow us to wait in a patient room for the results.

Twenty years later I can see the dismissiveness and institutional racism in the nurse's actions, but back then I was so grateful to have completed my master's degree and to have made it that far in life.[1] I think I was just doing enough just to make it through the situation, just enough to make it through every day. I hadn't planned on having a child then, but I naively and arrogantly believed at the time

---

1. See P. R. Lockhart, "What Serena Williams's Scary Childbirth Story Says about Medical Treatment of Black Women: Black Women Are Often Dismissed or Ignored by Medical Care Providers. Williams Wasn't an Exception," vox.com, January 11, 2018. https://www .vox.com/identities/2018/1/11/16879984/serena-williams-childbirth-scare-black-women.

that I would be fine because I wasn't a teenager and I had completed my education. With the best of intentions, I had been so trained as a Black girl growing up in poverty on the South Side of Chicago not to get pregnant and to complete my education. Little did I know that my so-called success and *ed-u-ma-ca-tion* only increased my mortality risk and the likelihood that I would miscarry, and that I was more likely to die from complications from pregnancy and childbirth.[2] I wondered if my White doctors and nurses understood this fact and if they even cared.

Once the nurse returned with the results, it seemed that because I had not yet made it to the first trimester, I wasn't worthy of seeing a doctor and waiting in an actual patient room. Apparently, my human chorionic gonadotropin (hCG) levels were not high enough for the length of time that I had been without a period, which was told to me and my sister in the public waiting room. We were not afforded the human dignity of privacy. I kept asking questions, and finally we were escorted to a waiting room, where a White female nurse did an ultrasound. It was confirmed that the fetus was dead or, in their words, "nonviable." The nurse also informed me that fetal loss in the first trimester is so normal that they, the medical establishment, don't even consider it an issue or problem unless a woman experiences three miscarriages in a row. It was all so very nonchalant and matter-of-fact that I felt like I maybe had overreacted. Maybe I did something wrong. The nurse explained that the

---

2. "The infant mortality rate for black babies is twice that for whites. But this is not a poverty story. Babies born to well educated, middle-class black mothers are more likely to die before their first birthday than babies born to poor white mothers with less than a high school education." See Richard V. Reeves and Dayna Bowen Matthew, "Social Mobility Memos: Six Charts Showing Race Gaps within the American Middle Class," Brookings.com, October 21, 2016. https://www.brookings.edu/blog/social-mobility-memos/2016/10/21/6 -charts-showing-race-gaps-within-the-american-middle-class/ Also see K. C. Schoendorf and C. J. R. Hogue, "Mortality among Infants of Black as Compared with White College-Educated Parents," *New England Journal of Medicine* 326, no. 23 (1992): 1522–27.

uterus and body would naturally expel the fetus, including tissue, and if it did not expel from the body in a couple of weeks, I was to return to the doctor.

I felt like I was in a daze and that a cruel trick had been played on me. I had spent more than sixteen years, since sixth grade, making sure that I didn't have a baby, that I didn't stink—as my sixth-grade teacher had warned us girls during "the talk" about our periods and wearing deodorant—and working hard to outlive my membership in the sixth-grade brown birds math group, as opposed to the red cardinals and blue jays math groups. Here, sixteen years later, in 1998, I had been responsible, I got *ed-u-macated*, fell in love, and now—finally—wanted to have a baby, and my body and the Universe were, like, "Fuck You!" The next week on Wednesday, which would have been the first day of my graduate writing program, I felt a quick tearing inside my belly and rushed to the bathroom. I missed my first class of the semester, a fiction class—the novel— and I spent that evening sitting long periods on the toilet with the steady sound of skin and blood clots dropping and flopping into water to keep me company. Even after all that, I was still in love with that skinny Black guy named for Jesus, and I still wanted to have his babies.

• • •

Maybe my miscarriage was a punishment, and I wondered if Black women could have it all: babies, education, a career, and love.

• • •

Before I became pregnant in 1998, my momma came to me in a dream, as she often did in the year after her sudden death in 1997 at the age of forty-nine. On one visit she told me about men, "that God will choose." I had no clue what the hell she was talking about, but when my current love interest at the time, Sphincter Muscle,

Sphinc, or Satan II, for short, started complaining of someone beating him in the head at night and waking him out of his sleep, I knew it was my momma. It was funny as hell to see how scared his community-dick-having-self was, but it still took me a couple of months to leave his trifling ass, because the sex was really good. From my late teens through my twenties, I had several relationships, had experienced my own loves, and watched the loves of family members disintegrate, and I knew and believed then, unequivocally, that I did not want to have any children.

• • •

"You will never find a husband and get married!" my grandma would yell at me when I, twelve years old and knowing it all, complained about my required daily chores of cleaning her house, which included the dreaded vacuum. My mother would send me and my older sister to stay with my grandma during the summers of the late eighties. I now realize it was another birth control strategy and to keep us away from what she feared could happen to latchkey kids in the summer streets of Chicago, latchkey Black girls home alone. It's ironic to think that my mother and her mother, Grandma, actually believed that it was harder for two preteen Black girls to get pregnant living in a small southern Illinois town in the middle of nowhere instead of on the South Side of Chicago with too much time on your hands.

"I don't want to get married and have a husband!" I would yell back at my grandma when she chastised me for not wanting to be her maid and clean her house every day.

My grandma would just look at me and shake her head. She really believed that she was living the life, and from her viewpoint I guess it made sense. She was born and raised in the Great Depression, and I can't imagine how dangerous it must have been for a pretty Black girl growing up in a small mining town run through by train tracks in southern Illinois in the 1930s and 1940s. As my grandma explained, she worked, cooked, took care of the kids, and cleaned the house, and my Pawpaw worked, paid the bills, fixed stuff around the house, kept the garden, and drank at the VFW every night. I do mean every night.

She and Pawpaw had five kids, and the oldest child, Mark Anthony, was stillborn. I knew this from as long as I could remember because my mother always talked about her stillborn brother, Mark. My momma so loved Mark that she named my baby brother, Ronnie, after him, but she ended up changing his name from Mark to my father's name, Ronald, because my father (Satan I) threw a stone-cold fit. Although my father had completely abandoned the family by the time that my baby brother was born, and even went so far as to tell people that my brother Ronnie wasn't his, my father still expected my mother to name her last and fifth child after him and not her dead stillborn brother. I was only eight years old then, but I understood. I wanted Momma not to cave to my father, but she did. It was like my father believed he owned my momma, her uterus, and what came out of it, even when he treated her and us, his children, like shit.

I guess it was hard because when my brother, Ronnie, was born, he looked like my father literally spit him out. I guess my father was my first relationship with a Sphincter Muscle. I could not understand a world where a man could marry a woman, have five kids with her, and walk away from her and his own kids and lead a life as if those kids did not come out of his nut sac, as if their mother who carried them in her body for nine months and pushed them out of her vagina did not exist. Where they do that at? Now you know why I, initially, was not down for the baby thing. That shit is just jacked up, and I had (have) issues, and I was never going to make myself that vulnerable to another human being.

• • •

Having grown up the second oldest of five kids and raised by a single mother, I experienced one of the best forms of birth control that exist. I was a mother of three kids at the age of eight. There were three siblings born after me, and by age eight, I was cooking, cleaning, changing diapers, and babysitting my sisters and brother because my mother had to go to work during the day to provide for us. By this time, my father had completely abandoned the family. I could count on one hand how many times from age eight through eighteen that I actually saw my father in a year's time, and just because I saw him didn't mean that he recognized and acknowledged me or my siblings as his children in those moments.

As experienced by most single mothers, particularly women of color, our father's physical abandonment of the family instantly left us in poverty. Although my mother worked tirelessly to keep a roof over our heads, there were many days when we went without basic necessities like heat, water, electricity, and sufficient food. I lived those ten years after my father left the house bearing witness to my mother's simultaneous suffering and tenacity, as a result of my father's betrayal and her structural social position as a single Black woman parent living in the urban North in the United States. I watched my mother's body become emaciated as she continually took the smallest piece of fried chicken at dinner to ensure that her five growing children had enough food. She wore coats and boots years beyond their physical utility in the bitter cold and windy Chicago winters because she spent what little money she had on warm clothes and boots for her growing kids. At night, she made us put on our winter coats and boots and squeeze in tight together on our only couch, and then she placed blankets over us in the hope that our small bodies would not freeze during the night in the below-zero winter weather, because our heat had been cut off for nonpayment. And when my period first started at the age of twelve, she screamed on a regular basis for my first year of bleeding, "You can get pregnant now!"—instead of the ideal *Pretty in Pink* Molly Ringwald Black girl experience that I really wanted.

Then, I believed and was resentful that I never had a chance to be a little girl or a teenager. Instead, while my mother was constantly making preemptive stealth moves and running rescue missions to ensure that her five babies lived beyond the womb despite the personal, historical, and socioeconomic conditions that forced the contrary on her daily, I played mother and father to myself and to my baby brother and sisters.

• • •

There is one Christmas photo after my father left the family and my mother had given birth to Ronnie the previous summer. My mother is wearing a white dress, and our backs are to the kitchen door because we don't have a tree or gifts for this Christmas. We have pretty dresses, we have a new baby brother, we don't have enough food, and we have love. I can't remember who took the photo, but I am 100 percent sure that it was not my father.

I have looked at the photo a million times over the years, and I always assumed that it was a happy time because for the most part, it was a happy memory for me. In the picture, my sisters and I are smiling Black girls, not recognizing or understanding at the time our momma's pain, suffering, strength, and sacrifice. It would be later after my mother's death in 1997 that my momma's mother, my grandma, would let a big-ass bone fall out of her mouth to tell us that Ronnie had been a twin. That while pregnant and going through the stress of my father's infidelity, abandonment, and financial struggles, my momma miscarried my baby brother's brother.

It was not until I had my own children that I looked at the photo again and could see how emaciated and tired my momma really was, while my sisters and I stood in front of her body, taking from it. That in its stance, although weary, her body was an unwavering foundation of our full Black girls' beauty and happiness of what all we knew, even in our poverty, as we wore our beautifully white detailed frilly dresses that Momma had sewn by hand, every stitch filled with the best of love, devotion, courage, and strength that she could give us.

• • •

"Don't you ever let a man do to you what your father did to me," my mother would preach to us daily until I left home for college at the age of seventeen, and you best believe that by high school I had Planned Parenthood on speed-dial, and I knew the quickest CTA bus route to the nearest clinic. Although I didn't fully understand it then, my mother was trying to tell me in her own way and in the words that she understood that my ability to have agency and control over my uterus, my choice to procreate, and my mental, emotional, and physical health would directly connect to my ability to access my dreams, autonomy, liberty, citizenship, and equity as a Black woman living in this world.

• • •

I have a tilted, retroverted uterus. Although a uterus can become tilted for many reasons, some women are born with a tipped uterus. From my first pap smear as a teenager, once doctors discovered that my uterus was retroverted, they treated me like a specimen in a cage. With permission of course, OB-GYNs would call in their colleagues and students for an opportunity to *see* my uterus, live and direct, shifted back as a result of heredity. My younger sister, the third child, has a bicornuate, or heart-shaped, uterus, and she successfully carried and birthed two healthy children. Having a heart-shaped uterus is genetic too. Like a preening large cat, I used to think that my uterus was special, until I learned that one out of every five women has a tilted uterus, and it is really a fairly common physical condition.

In the essay "Crooked Room" from *Sister Citizen: Shame, Stereotypes, and Black Women in America*, Melissa Harris-Perry notes that "black women are standing in a crooked room, and they have to figure out which way is up. Bombarded with warped images of their humanity, some black women tilt and bend themselves to fit the distortion." She goes on to argue that despite the public and political actions of Black women that may contradict stereotypes, the reality is that "it can be hard to stand up straight in a crooked room."[3]

Maybe God tilted my uterus because S/HE understood the social economic challenges and contradictions that I would face as a Black woman born into this crooked world that makes it hard for Black and Brown women to stand straight, to find equilibrium. My uterus's slight tilt, like the universal Black greeting of the head nod with an explicit or implicit "What's up?" allowed me the ability to find equilibrium despite the constant distortions caused by the intersectionality of gendered, racial, and class oppression that I and my body, my uterus, and my dead, born, and unborn Black babies have experienced.[4] The tilt in my uterus might be the only physical thing keeping me and other women, especially Brown and Black women, upright.

· · ·

---

3. Melissa Harris-Perry, "Crooked Room," in *Sister Citizen: Shame, Stereotypes, and Black Women in America* (New Haven, Conn.: Yale University Press, 2011), 28–50.
4. Musa Okwonga, "The Nod: A Subtle Lowering of the Head You Give to Another Black Person in an Overwhelmingly White Place," *Medium*, October 16, 2014. https://medium.com/matter/the-nod-a-subtle-lowering-of-the-head-to-another-black-person-in-an-overwhelmingly-white-place-e12bfa0f833f.

A year after I left Sphinc (Satan II) in 1998, I met a Black skinny man who told me that his name, Emmanuel, means that "God is with us." All I could think about was that he had the prettiest set of white teeth and the kindest brown eyes that I had ever seen. He was the gentlest person that I had ever met. Emmanuel explained that he initially wanted to be a priest, so he was right with God. When he smiled at me for the first time and asked if he could carry my book bag back to my apartment, I really knew that Jesus was indeed with us, as my ovaries actually tingled for real for real, and I knew that I was in trouble. All my years of shit-talking about wanting to have absolutely no kids went out the front door. Three months later, after meeting a Black man with a name that meant Jesus is with us, I was pregnant at age twenty-eight, overeducated, unmarried, un-employed, in love, full of hope, and so excited to have a baby. For the first time in my life, I felt free, and that I could do anything that I wanted.

• • •

That August summer night in 2000 in the Iowa suburb, I didn't rec-ognize the Black man in the brown slacks and sweater that stood by and shook my bed while I slept. I jumped up, turned on the lights, and went to the bathroom. In my family, Spirits only came to visit to bring messages, primarily death. I couldn't go back to sleep and waited for Emmanuel to arrive from work. After making sure that he had showered and placed his uniform and shoes in a hermet-ically sealed plastic trash bag left outside the bedroom, I allowed him to enter the room. With a great deal of hubris, I suggested to Emmanuel that he phone home to make sure that everyone was all right, because I believed that I recognized every Spirit that had ever approached me. Since I didn't recognize the Black man in brown pants, it must have been a visit for Emmanuel.

Although I had been cramping in my lower abdomen over the past week and my OB-GYN had diagnosed me with uterine fibroids, telling me that women carried full healthy babies to term perfectly with uterine fibroids, it wasn't in the realm of my imagination to even consider that my almost-five-month-old baby in my stomach could die—again.

The next morning Emmanuel and I woke to start our drive to Minnesota, as we were moving there, and I was headed back to graduate school to complete my program. That morning I had been experiencing painful cramping without any blood, and I called my OB-GYN clinic. I thought maybe that I should go to the emergency room, but neither Emmanuel nor I had any health insurance at the time.

I left an urgent message for the doctor.

He called me back.

"You can go to the emergency room, but they are only going to give you Tylenol and send you home. Just take Tylenol, and you will be fine," he said matter-of-factly. Although in great pain, I trusted the doctor and didn't go to the emergency room. I took Tylenol, and Emmanuel and I set out that day for our three- to four-hour drive to Minneapolis.

An hour south of the Minnesota border on Interstate 35, I felt a pop, and water gushed down my legs and pooled at my sandal-covered feet. I could hear myself screaming, "No! No! No! No!" thinking that if I said it loud enough it could stop the water from running out of my body.

Emmanuel pulled to the side of the road, and we decided that we would drive to the nearest hospital. When we arrived at the hospital, I told them that my water had broken.

I remember sitting in a wheelchair in the hallway as people walked past me like they did not want to touch me. People walked past me like they did not see me. I sat there in the wheelchair thinking that as long as I didn't stand up, water would not flow out of my uterus.

All the people in the hospital were White.

I just kept praying that the water, the amniotic fluid, remained in my womb.

When I finally was given a room while they asked for information about my OB-GYN, they called my doctor and waited for his response. I lay in the hospital bed and cried while Emmanuel held my hand. The nurses kept asking for the name of my primary physician, but I only had an OB-GYN.

As I write this essay, I realize that I was college educated, twenty-eight years old, and I didn't have a primary doctor. I didn't see a doctor regularly or yearly unless there was something wrong. I didn't go to the doctor unless I had to. Going to the doctor was never an enjoyable or comfortable experience for me as a woman of color, and the one moment when I really needed a doctor, it felt like I didn't have one, because the OB-GYN seemed to just be going through the motions. The OB-GYN made me feel like he didn't care about me. I wondered if the OB-GYN was married, and if his wife was pregnant with fibroids and cramping would he have told her to take Tylenol, or would he have insisted that she go to the emergency room.

I don't remember much about the exam in the emergency room, but doctors were in agreement that my water had broken; however, I was not going into labor as they expected. It was then that I finally realized that my stomach cramping had stopped.

A doctor from my clinic, not my OB-GYN from that same clinic, finally called the emergency room, and he, with a kind voice, advised me to return to Iowa and be admitted to the hospital where the clinic was located to see if the amniotic fluid would fill back up in the sac. The doctor said that sometimes the fluid builds back up. I was hopeful, and Emmanuel and I returned to the hospital near the clinic, and I was admitted.

I was in the hospital for seven days. During those days I can only remember feeling the baby move and me crying. It was my first time to feel the baby move because I was close to twenty weeks. The doctor told me that I could feel the baby move because there was no longer any fluid in the amniotic sac. I was constantly worried that the baby was feeling pain and could not breathe properly because there was so much fluid loss. After a week, the hospital doctors realized that my amniotic sac was not going to refill with amniotic fluid, so they gave me the option of inducing labor or having a D&C. After feeling the baby for that entire week, I couldn't imagine them doing a D&C on the baby, so we opted for induction. It was then, after a week of crying, waiting, and drinking as much water as one could imagine, that I realized that my original OB-GYN doctor from the clinic never visited me in the hospital. He never came to the hospital room, and he never even called.

It was then that a different doctor, not mine at the clinic, told me that all the time I had been cramping and experiencing what I felt was like really bad period cramps and the baby just growing, I was really in labor. I didn't know it because I had never given birth to a baby, and my clinic OB-GYN did not inform me of this. My uterine fibroids were intramural, submucosal, and subserosal. In other words, the tumors were inside my uterus, embedded into the walls of my uterus, and on the outside walls of my uterus, and they put pressure on the amniotic sac until it burst because there wasn't enough room inside my uterus for both the growing fibroids and the growing baby from where the placenta was attached.[5]

---

5. According to Elizabeth A. Stewart et al., "Multiple lines of evidence suggest that uterine fibroids have a disproportional effect on African-American women. African-American women have a higher cumulative risk of uterine fibroids, a threefold greater incidence and relative risk of fibroids, and an earlier age of onset. In addition, African-American women

Because of my uterine fibroids, I should have been classified as a high-risk pregnancy, and when I called the clinic doctor the night before we left for our trip to Minnesota complaining of really bad cramping, the clinic doctor should have told me to go to the nearest emergency room immediately in order to try to stop my labor, as I was automatically high risk for miscarriage. You can do everything you are supposed to do, and stuff can still go left.

I was placed in a labor-and-delivery room. The room seemed really empty as there were no extra accessories: no infant bed with a warmer, no baby blankets, no bassinet, no scale, no fetal monitors, no maternity kits, etc. This was a room for a dead baby with the barest of essentials, as the doctor had told us that the baby would not survive the birth. Even then, I was still hoping.

I naively believed that the labor would not be difficult, because I rationalized that the baby was so small. What damage could an almost-twenty-week fetus do to the body?

I was given a morphine drip and a Pitocin drip. At first it wasn't that bad, but I quickly reached my maximum drug allowance on the morphine, and it started to hurt really badly.

"It hurts, it hurts, it hurts" were the only words I had for Emmanuel.

It was like it was not happening to me, and I was floating above the room just watching it and recording it in my memory for future recall. Like a person under duress, I knew my job was just to merely get through it. I was used to the worst things happening and knowing how to survive and appear normal in spite of them.

---

are 2.4 times more likely to undergo hysterectomy and have a 6.8-fold increase of undergoing uterine-sparing myomectomy. At the time of hysterectomy, African-American women have higher uterine weights, more fibroids, a higher likelihood of preoperative anemia, and more severe pelvic pain. Data also suggests that African-American women may have biologically distinct disease." Elizabeth A. Stewart, Wanda K. Nicholson, Linda Bradley, and Bijan J. Borah, "The Burden of Uterine Fibroids for African-American Women: Results of a National Survey," *Journal of Women's Health* 22, no. 10 (2013): 807–16.

"Can you press again? It really hurts," I asked Emmanuel.

"You've reached your maximum dose," he told me.

Once I was fully dilated, the baby came, and she was a girl.

"I can see her chest moving! See! She's breathing! She's breathing!" I told the doctor as he held her, and I watched him gently come over to me and press his thumb over her chest reminding me that she was too small for any instruments to aid her. I think I thought if I looked at her hard enough and concentrated that she would come back to life.

She was so tiny and beautiful. I just kept smelling her because she smelled so good and so different. I had never smelled anything like it. She smelled like something from another world, and it smelled so good. My baby did not stink, and I couldn't believe that she came out of me and that I smelled that good on the inside. Even in that moment I wondered why my sixth-grade teacher had taught us that Black girls stink. I knew then that she was a liar. Since my baby came out of me smelling so good, then I must be good, too. I just wanted her to be good with me and to stay with me. I think I kept her blankets for more than ten years, just to take them out of their special box to smell them every now and then.

We called the priest to give last rites, and when he entered the room, we showed him our baby, who to us was the most beautiful girl in the world. The White Catholic priest physically recoiled as if he had seen something repulsive. I thought, "I'm Catholic, and Emmanuel is Catholic, named after Jesus. Why wouldn't he want to baptize our baby girl and give her last rites?"

The hardest was leaving the hospital and leaving her there. I kept wanting to go back and to look and touch her body, and I did. I knew it was not healthy, but I just wanted to keep looking at her and touching her just one more time. I couldn't stop myself. We took pictures, but I kept feeling like I would forget her, and it is the worst feeling in the world to believe that you are going to forget what your child looks like because you know that you won't see her face again. We finally decided to have her cremated because as students we were not attached to any place, and I could not imagine burying her in a place where we didn't live and then she would be there alone and all by herself. Our daughter was cremated and placed in a brass urn, which I still have placed on an altar today with pictures of my mother, grandmothers, auntie, and uncle, all of whom have passed.

• • •

Sylvia Browne, a prominent psychic, was scheduled to come to the Twin Cities in 2001, and unbeknownst to Emmanuel, I splurged and bought tickets for us to see her. Pregnant again, I was about twenty weeks along, and we were living in an apartment in South Minneapolis. We were both working and in school. The arena where Browne was speaking was full to capacity, and Emmanuel and I were seated on the main floor in the back. By this time, we had been together for more than two years, and he was used to my fascination with Spirits. Plus, he was named after Jesus, so how could he not be as well?

That night Sylvia Browne held a lottery for all ticket holders to choose what lucky ones would go to the stage to ask her a question directly. I was not one of the lucky ones. I had two chances because Emmanuel told me that he would have given me his ticket if his number was called. I told ya'll he was sweet. Anyway, Browne led the entire auditorium through a guided meditation, and she advised everyone to individually ask in their heads the question that we would like our Higher Power, in my case God/Universe, to answer for us.

"Will my baby make it past twenty-five weeks?"

"Will my baby make it past twenty-five weeks?"

"Please God, will my baby make it past twenty-five weeks?" I kept asking this question over and over again in my head like a mantra, a prayer. Although these questions were a part of my guided meditation with Sylvia Browne in that moment in the auditorium there in St. Paul sitting next to Emmanuel, this question had been my obsession since we found out that we were pregnant again.

• • •

"You call us anytime for any concerns that you have about your pregnancy. It's better to be safe than sorry, and our job is to make you feel at ease," is what the clinic nurse in 2001 told me. This time, we had an OB-GYN who diagnosed me as a high-risk pregnancy, and I received the additional and needed medical care, compassion, and concern relative to my medical condition and risks.[6] My OB-GYN was part of a clinic that specifically served women of color and understood the unique risks and disparities relative to women of color and pregnancy: hypertensive disorders, diabetes, fibroids, education, and poverty.[7] They made me feel like they cared, and they listened to me and responded to my questions and needs. I knew that there were never any guarantees, but Emmanuel and I felt confident in our health care and pregnancy this time around. We felt that we were receiving care from experts who met our medical needs and actually cared about the success of our pregnancy, birth, and child.

• • •

---

6. Kiera Butler, "A Surprisingly Simple Way Black Women Can Reduce Pregnancy Risks," *MotherJones* July/August 2018. https://www.motherjones.com/politics/2018/08/simple-way-reduce-risk-black-pregnancy-premature-birth/.
7. Linda Villarosa, "Why America's Black Mothers and Babies Are in a Life-or-Death Crisis: The Answer to the Disparity in Death Rates Has Everything to Do with the Lived Experience of Being a Black Woman in America," *New York Times Magazine*, April 11, 2018. https://www.nytimes.com/2018/04/11/magazine/black-mothers-babies-death-maternal-mortality.html.

The guided mediation with Sylvia Browne ended, I felt refreshed, and Emmanuel and I drove back to our basement apartment in South Minneapolis.

That night I was awakened by someone shaking the bed. We had graduated to a full bed, and I was lying flat on my back, and my right side was on the edge. I looked to my right, and there was the same Black man with the brown pants and sweater that I first saw in the summer of 2000. He had returned, but this time he was not alone. There was someone standing next to him to his right, dressed in a glowing white robe like a Roman toga.

Again, I seemed not to lift my eyes high enough to see their faces. The person in the white robe had an open book in his hand, and he lifted his right hand and pointed directly to my stomach while the Black man in brown pants looked at the man in white. The Black man in brown pants then jumped into my stomach, and my whole body shook and vibrated from my tummy throughout my entire frame, and a feeling of complete peace and knowingness fell over me. I knew then that I had watched my child's soul enter her body and that the baby I was carrying, right then and there in 2001, was going to be all right.

I looked to my left and saw that Emmanuel, Jesus, had slept through the entire thing. I realized in that moment that back when my bed shook during that hot, muggy August night in 2000, my daughter's Spirit had come to tell me, "Mommy, not yet." She was letting me know that it wasn't her time but was trying to explain to me that she would return, and on that night in 2001 her soul did just that.

• • •

As bad-ass as I pretended and wanted to be, I decided that I couldn't be a fifth-generation recovering Catholic with a Catholic baby daddy named Jesus and not get married. With an eight-month-full belly, Emmanuel and I were married at the Hennepin County Courthouse. My baby brother, Ronnie, and my sister with the heart-shaped uterus stood as witnesses. Our daughter was born thirty-three days later at nine pounds and twenty-one inches long. I prayed during my twelve hours and seventeen minutes of labor that I would see my mother, but I didn't, and I named my daughter after her anyway.

Making the
Invisible Visible

Mapping Racial Housing Covenants in South Minneapolis

Fourteen years ago when my realtor asked me to wait in the
Nokomis Public Library at the corner of the block while he met with
the White homeowners of a 1925 cottage bungalow two-bedroom
house that my husband and I wanted to make an offer on, I didn't
give it much thought. I trusted him. We'd been looking at homes
in South Minneapolis for months, and every homeowner of every
house that we viewed south of Forty-sixth Street, east of Port-
land Avenue and west of Hiawatha Avenue, never accepted our
bids, even when my husband and I seemed to be the only buyers
making an offer. When my realtor asked me to wait in the library,
I didn't think about the first time that we actually saw the bungalow: we drove by it, several times, at night. I only thought about the
softly lit wood-framed piano windows that I could make out from
our slowly moving car, despite the home's worn roof and peeling
stucco exterior. After we viewed the inside of the home during the
day while the homeowners were at work, the high ceilings, hard-
wood floors, and white and aqua blue honeycomb bathroom tile

outweighed the all-too-real work that the home needed, what my realtor called "tender love and care." To me and my husband with our thirteen-month-old daughter, the cottage bungalow was just the right size in the modest, quiet Keewaydin neighborhood, which is walking distance from Lake Nokomis and city biking and walking trails, with a decent school district and park recreation center. And most important, it was affordable on my new teacher's salary.

After fifteen minutes, my realtor, all smiles, returned to the library with a signed purchased agreement from the homeowners, who had signed the agreement without ever meeting me and my husband. After moving in, I realized two things: one, that my neighbors were the kindest people that anyone would ever have the pleasure of meeting; and two, that my husband and I were the only Black family on our block.

What did my realtor know that he did not have the heart to tell me or that I did not have the heart to see myself?

According to mappingprejudice.org, a map reveals "demographic [racial] patterns [of segregation] that remain in place in Minneapolis today." Mapping Prejudice is a database building project housed in the John R. Borchert Map Library at the University of Minnesota Libraries. According to Kirsten Delegard, director of the project, she and her team are historians and geographers working within the digital humanities analyzing old data with new technology to create a variety of outputs, which include better understanding of past and present systemic structures in Minneapolis, such as housing segregation and racism. This mapping project is the first ever in the United States to comprehensively map racial covenants on such a large scale. Through the use of optical character recognition software, 90 percent of the project's work is building the database itself, and as a result, the project is always looking for volunteers from the community to electronically search the deeds for racial covenants. Penny Petersen, a writer and property records specialist for the project, notes the importance of the project being directly engaged with the community as a partner, which keeps the methodology and outcomes transparent and accountable. The very Minneapolis citizens affected by the data can be a part of contributing to the construction of the database. Ryan Mattke, map and geospatial information librarian and libraries liaison to the project, says that the database can become a launch point from which people can then ask their own questions.

According to Kevin Ehrman-Solberg, project manager and geographic information science specialist, the project converts information from historic Minneapolis city property deeds that are digitized images into a database that includes spatial variables. The variables include racially restricted language like "described premises shall not be sold, mortgaged, or leased to or occupied by any person or persons other than members of the Caucasian race," along with additions, lot, block, document numbers, and other housing deed data. When searched, selected variables in the database can spatially show how, where, and when racial segregation was constructed into Minneapolis housing and subsequent neighborhoods in the first half of the twentieth century. Like many U.S. cities in the urban north, these racialized covenants in Minneapolis legally prevented non-White, primarily Blacks, from purchasing homes in certain Minneapolis neighborhoods. Although the Fair Housing Act of 1968 outlawed de jure racial covenants and redlining, a different form of discrimination ensuing from and cumulative to racial covenants worked to structurally create and embed the de facto racial identity, housing segregation, and subsequent racial disparities in Minneapolis and in the United States that remain today.[1] Ryan Mattke notes that when spatial maps of racial covenants

---

1. See the "Federal Fair Lending Regulations and Statutes" of the Fair Housing Act: "Redlining is the practice of denying a creditworthy applicant a loan for housing in a certain neighborhood even though the applicant may otherwise be eligible for the loan. The

in Minneapolis overlay other Minneapolis maps, especially maps of racial disparities in health, education, incarceration, and wealth, etc., there are correlations. What does it mean when the patterns of racial discrimination in housing can also predict individual life expectancy, education, incarceration, and net wealth, among other things? In Minneapolis, through racial covenants, people of color were systematically disenfranchised and not allowed access to the privilege of accumulating wealth and U.S. American identity through housing, which still has devastating (reverberating) impacts today.

Segregated neighborhoods negatively affected Blacks and Whites. Blacks experienced the subsequent social disparities at micro and macro levels, and Whites developed implicit bias at a conscious and subconscious level, which worked to solidify a racial social hierarchy and identity constructions of people, places, and spaces, so that long after racial covenants were outlawed they still are in effect in Minneapolis, as in my neighborhood of Nokomis. Because the history of racial covenants is largely unknown, it remains invisible and the segregation of people of color in the predominantly White spaces of the city of Minneapolis is normalized. I can see Black people in North Minneapolis, but not around Lake of the Isles or Nokomis.

Ultimately, Mapping Prejudice becomes a resource, and the spatially mapped answers to questions asked can be placed in the hands of activists, lawmakers, community members, and other stakeholders to positively affect education, public policy, and, hopefully, change, transformation, and equity.

The legacy of racial covenants in Minneapolis is racial segregation, and the negative effects of structural racism in the city and

---

term refers to the presumed practice of mortgage lenders of drawing red lines around portions of a map to indicate areas or neighborhoods in which they do not want to make loans." https://www.federalreserve.gov/boarddocs/supmanual/cch/fair_lend_fhact.pdf.

state are widespread. According to *24/7 Wall St.*, Minnesota has the second-largest racial disparity in the United States, with 21.7 percent of Blacks owning their own homes compared to 76 percent of Whites.[2] In a sense, Mapping Prejudice is a form of time travel that is working to change the collective narrative of the past, because it gives us a different, better understanding of that past. Kirsten Delegard and her team are creating a database resource and a public service to Minnesota, which will unlock an aspect of structural racism that very few of us understand but, more important, that few of us have the patience and desire to understand. Housing is key, as housing most likely determines future education, employment, incarceration, and net worth or wealth. A home is not just the place where we live: it is a place where we achieve and grow into the U.S. American dream for ourselves and our families.

After fourteen years, to my knowledge, after watching homes be bought and sold, sometimes on the market and many times not, we are still the only Black family on our block.

---

2. See Michael B. Sauter, "Black and White Inequality in All 50 States," *24/7 Wall St.*, August 18, 2017.

What's Understood Don't Need to Be Explained

It was on a Tuesday, just two weeks into the fall 2017 semester, when Brent P. Ahlers, a White male security guard, was shot and wounded while patrolling a heavily wooded part of the St. Catherine University grounds. It was two months and a year past the shooting death of Philando Castile by a St. Anthony policeman and the start of my second year as one of the few full-time African American tenure-track faculty members in the entire university. As I sat in my early-twentieth-century, high-ceilinged office, romantically gazing out my large picture window, I wondered if it was the same security guard who mistook me and my Tanzanian American husband for janitors a little over a year ago as we excitedly worked late into the night to move me into my new office.

WCCO and the Minneapolis *Star Tribune* reported that Ahlers told St. Paul police that he encountered a Black man around 9:25 that night. Ahlers told the police that he confronted a Black male who was wearing "a navy-blue sweatshirt with a short afro" and that the Black man shot him in the shoulder, ran through the trees, jumped over a six-foot-plus fence, and then disappeared.

After hearing the story, I did the mental self-check that most institutionally traumatized Black people in America who are always seen as naturally suspect do.

Am I Black? Yes.

Do I wear a short Afro? Yes.

Do I own a gun? No.

Was I in the campus woods on Tuesday? No.

Do I own a navy-blue sweatshirt? I wear a nice navy-blue top sometimes, but I'm sure it can't be mistaken for a navy-blue sweatshirt. Right?

Can I scale and jump a six-foot-plus fence? Hell, no!

Will they think it was me? Only time will tell.

In response to Ahlers's initial report, the *New York Daily News* reported that "55 officers, a Minnesota State Patrol helicopter, and four K-9 units" responded to the crime scene to apprehend one person. The university was put on lockdown while law enforcement officials searched for the "hostile shooter" until an all-clear was given. All the while, the historic and highly racially segregated St. Paul neighborhoods of Highland Park and Macalester–Groveland and their various businesses and schools were on high alert. According to a *CBS Minnesota* report, the shooting incident "had residents . . . fearful that a suspect was on the loose and [they] . . . could be victimized at any moment" by a Black man running and hiding in neighborhoods that are more than 79 percent White and 90 percent White, respectively, as a direct legacy of racial covenants.

By half past midnight, the St. Paul Police said that Ahlers was at a local hospital with non–life-threatening injuries, and according to the *Star Tribune*, "no one had been arrested, but there was an active search for the suspect." It was an expected, micro (Minnesota) and macro (national) narrative. A foreign unlawful Black body perpetuates violence, makes life unsafe for lawful White bodies, and that Black body must be caught and stopped by any means necessary, i.e., deadly local and state law enforcement.

No one publicly seemed to question the narrative for at least the first twenty-four hours. As Rachel Siegel reported in the September 15, 2017, edition of the *Washington Post*, almost three and half hours after the event the St. Paul Police released tweets that said the "search has concluded; no suspect located; investigation ongoing." Internally, the police were already doubting the security guard's story, and as a result they never released an official statement that the suspect was a Black male. However, "audio from police scanner traffic posted by MN Police Clips was widely shared on social media." That audio included identifiers such as the fabricated suspect's race, navy-blue sweatshirt, and Afro. The official St. Paul Police tweets never specifically stated that there was no threat from a Black male assailant or that a Black male assailant did not exist.

I thanked God that my husband was not in the neighborhood that night, coming to pick me up from the university or going to the Kowalski's grocery store that we frequent in St. Paul. Imagine what could have happened to any Black person unlucky enough to be anywhere in that neighborhood during those initial hours after "the shooting" had been reported.

The following day, students and community members were understandably shaken and needed to be calmed and counseled. The entire school met in the campus chapel with the university administrators for support and answers. As the chapel overflowed, I, like many faculty, staff, and administrators, gave up my seat on the church pew for students and took my place standing along the back wall of the sanctuary with my colleagues. As we watched and listened to university officials deftly field questions from frightened and concerned students, they answered that "sometimes gifts come wrapped in ugly packages."

• • •

"Taiyon, don't crucify yourself on a small cross" is what a well-meaning White male supervisor and mentor once told me when I sought him out for advice on how to handle an inequitable workplace experience I was having. I was being low-key bullied by a White male employee who was my counterpart but seemed to have an ongoing problem with my having more education and consequently earning a higher salary than he did, although we held the same job title.

I know.

I should have known better.

I wanted to believe.

I wanted to believe that my education could really work and keep me safe from institutional racial injustice.

"Your education is the one thing they can never take away from you," my momma constantly preached to me and my siblings growing up on Chicago's South Side. She neglected to talk to us about the things that they *could* take away.

The job with the White boss was my attempt at achieving the American Dream through employment assimilation, so I had accepted a career where the dress code required female employees to wear pantyhose. I don't think at the time my boss knew that I was a first-generation college-educated and a fifth-generation Black Catholic woman in resistance and recovery. I answered his deadpan crucifixion statement in response to my complaints of racial discrimination and sexual harassment with belly-felt hilarious loud laughter that moved into quiet nervousness and a reflection that permeated my entire body. It's a feeling that comes when you know that what you just experienced has marked your whole person, physical and spiritual, like annual growth rings marking a tree.

My White boss's advice at the time assumed that my workplace crucifixion was inevitable, yet he implied that I had a choice in how I would sacrifice my Black life for others. He was saying, "Yes, Taiyon, what is happening to you in the workplace is not fair, it is wrong, but let this one go. You will have bigger fish to fry" (another Catholic reference), meaning that some inequity and injustice is acceptable, maybe necessary for success and daily life in our societies, cultures, and institutions.

Was he saying that my direct experiences of racism, sexism, and other forms of oppression as a Black woman are necessary in order to maintain workplace (read: institutional, social) peace and order?

I left that White boss supervisor meeting feeling that one day there would be an injustice so big that I would pick up a really big cross for it, do the right thing, and eventually die.

Death on a cross for whose benefit?

Is this the gift?

Who's the recipient?

One lump or two?

I felt like the 1950s cartoon character Pete Puma when Bugs Bunny invites him for tea and asks him how many lumps he wants. Pete Puma is trusting and assumes that his host, Bugs Bunny, is offering him sugar to sweeten his tea. Instead, Pete Puma ends up being beaten in the head.

I left that job and returned to classroom teaching.

• • •

Many scholars believe that the tradition of gift giving started with the three kings who brought gifts to honor the birth of Christ. In the article "The History and Complexities of Gift Giving," Kristin Grant writes that it is based on culture, but most agree that gift giving is reciprocal and involves indebtedness. Ahlers's lying about a Black man shooting him to avoid the consequences of his illegal actions was a *gift* to himself and simultaneously a *gift* to the construction and perpetuation of Whiteness and White Supremacy, as Black in U.S. America is *always guilty* and *never free,* and White in U.S. America is *always right* and *full of liberty.* As a result, the cultural and institutional perpetuation of the racial stereotype of Black men as dangerous and violent becomes a *cross* and subsequent *gift* that just keeps on giving in St. Paul, greater Minnesota, and the larger American society as a necessary tradition since its onset.

In his book *Slavery and Social Death*, Orlando Patterson asserts that racialized slavery within the United States of America helped to define and shape what freedom meant to a new, young nation by possessing people (enslaved Black Africans and their descendants) who did not have freedom. Was the enslavement of Black Africans and their subsequent cross—their racialization, oppression, torture, and killing in America—an ugly package gift-wrapped for White Americans in order to define U.S. citizenship, freedom, and Whiteness, which takes priority over Black life? In this paradigm, how might one consider the inevitable (read: necessary) oppression of Black people in academia and other U.S. institutions that historically determine and measure the quality of life, freedom, and equity in the United States of America?

There is a better way to remove the obscuring illusion of institutionalized White supremacy to see the reality of Black people in America. We should accept that some Americans consciously and/or subconsciously have been socialized to believe that the direct or indirect social and/or literal death of Black people is central and necessary to their individual, financial, and national success and identity. In an 1820 letter about the conflicts of slavery and states' rights, Thomas Jefferson wrote to John Holmes that "justice is in one scale, and self-preservation in the other" when considering the then and now future dialectic of American democracy. Even Dan Patrick, lieutenant governor of Texas, as reported by Justine Coleman in *The Hill* on April 22, 2020, said, "There are more important things than living and that's saving this country for my children and grandchildren and saving this country for all of us" when asked about shutting down his state to reduce the spread of the deadly Covid-19 virus.

• • •

Considering that the death rate in America has exceeded four hundred thousand as of January 2021 and Black, Latinx, and Native Americans are twice as likely or more to die from Covid-19 than their White counterparts, it is highly problematic that the majority of Americans still don't see racial disparities in health care and life outcomes. What Lieutenant Governor Patrick was really saying was: the lives of my children and grandchildren are more important than the lives, safety, and health of Black, Latinx, and Native people. And letting Black, Latinx, and Native American people die (killing them) saves this country for *us*, not them. If Black and Brown people have to die of Covid-19 in order for me to generate revenue and save a way of life within a capitalist economy at all costs, then so be it. The cost is always the death of the Black and Brown body, and that body is the gift. So many White people in America from Thomas Jefferson to Dan Patrick to Minneapolis police officer Derek Chauvin are willing to take and accept that gift.

In order for American Whiteness and a White way of life to exist and be sustained, Black people, like George Floyd, must be literally and/or figuratively choked to death. Black children must drink leaded water, breathe mold from within segregated homes, and receive a substandard public education that tracks them into incarceration like sheep to slaughter. Black women must be strong, brilliant, and overqualified and work twice as hard just to receive no credit and less pay. They disproportionately remain in generational poverty, have a lower life expectancy than their White counterparts, are more likely to die from hypertension and other preventable diseases caused and exacerbated by sexism and racism, and on top of all of this, are told they are intimidating, difficult, and hard to work with because they dare try to thrive and survive. Black men can't run and walk openly in neighborhoods, they can't kneel during the national anthem, they can't use a twenty-dollar bill at the neighborhood corner store, but they are always suspected felons who can be choked to death for holding a loose cigarette, incarcerated without trial for three years on suspicion of stealing a backpack before committing suicide, and shot point-blank in the park for being a twelve-year-old boy and wanting to play with a plastic toy that looks like a gun.

And if you can't find an actual real Black person to kill, you can always just magically make one up.

The paradox of Minnesota being a "nice" place to live while having one of the largest racial disparities in the nation is actually an American paradox, as racial disparities today in the United States are worse than they were before the civil rights era. If the police state executions of Jamar Clark, Philando Castile, David Smith, Terrance Franklin, Travis Jordan, George Floyd, and Dolal Idd in Minnesota are any evidence, it seems the fears that Jefferson wrote about in 1820 were prophetical and material. Minnesotans like many Americans are still choosing Whiteness and the institutionalized social and literal death of Black people as the ritualized sacrifice that sustains them and maintains a *certain way (quality) of American life.* And they continue choosing their own self-preservation over justice, with the result being the real gift that keeps on giving, wrapped in ugly packages of oppressed Black life and death, no matter the gender or age, contorted and obscured as freedom celebrating liberty.

In the Catholic tradition, Jesus's gift to humankind was that he died on the cross for the sins of man, and he even asked his Father, God, to "forgive them for they know not what they do," after they betrayed and tortured Him. His death was very ugly, so the story goes, yet it is taught and celebrated as a gift to humankind.

Lord knows, it couldn't be me. Yet Sandra Bland said the same thing, and look what happened to her.

• • •

In the chapel, I was one of the few Black bodies in the space. I was so busy being compassionate toward the fear and anxiety of my students and other community members that I didn't think about their fear of Black bodies, especially my own Black body in St. Paul, Minnesota. I should have been just an associate professor in the English department. But after receiving that cross from Ahlers's lie, a gift that placed me on the periphery of the spectating crowd looking at the aftermath of a social lynching, I was just another witness to another ritualized murder of a Black body swinging from an institutional tree. How easily the situation can turn when you are the marginalized Black body in White-dominant spaces and institutions whose data in employment, student enrollment and matriculation, and experiences of BIPOC members mirror a larger system of racial, class, and gender apartheid.

I left the chapel before the program ended and spent the rest of the day grading papers in my office. Thursday morning, it was reported that Ahlers had actually shot himself, had completely fabricated the Black male suspect, and was arrested by St. Paul Police without incident. Ahlers was convicted on one count of misdemeanor for falsely reporting a crime to police, fired from the university, and sentenced to one year of probation during which he was required to attend a "Black men's group," with actual real Black men.

I know.

What are real Black men?

Real Black men are men that White people can easily imagine and still kill.

The sun setting, I looked out my office window over my plants and into the trees. Their swaying green leaves reminded me that this wasn't the first time and it wouldn't be the last time that Black bodies produced by White imagination would die like they did in poet Cornelius Eady's *Brutal Imagination*. I thought about how

You Can Miss Me with That, 'Cause Plantations Were Diverse, Too

If you would have told me when I first attended college that I would end up teaching as a career and vocation, I would have said that you must be out of your mind. Dude. For real. Statistically, I wasn't even supposed to pass my first-year composition course as a first-generation college student born and raised in the inner city of Chicago, and I didn't. Statistically, I wasn't even supposed to be a Black female tenured faculty writing instructor at a two-year college in Minnesota, but I am. For real, for real. Doe.[1]

When I attended a professional discipline-specific conference a couple of years back (much like the conference at which this essay was a presentation), I immediately felt an unease when I entered the convention venue, and at first I couldn't understand why. Attendees seemed outwardly nice, and I had been teaching writing at the college and university level for more than fifteen years. I had just completed my terminal degree in the field along with scoring a first-round job interview. By all accounts, it should have been good

---

1. See Marshawn Lynch, "I'm gon' get mine more than I get got, doe," YouTube.

times. But while I walked around the conference venue politely seeking gentle smiles, hellos, and nondescript informal greetings from those who were now my colleagues, I had a hard time meeting their eyes, and most of the attendees, who were socially, historically, and institutionally constructed as White, rarely met mine.

On the second day of the conference as I made my way to eat lunch, I sat at an empty table, and a Black woman came to my table and asked if she could sit and eat with me. I said, "Sure." It was then that I realized why I was uncomfortable at the conference. I re-remembered, I re-assessed, and I re-viewed back to the previous day when I first arrived. For the most part, I was among the few racially constructed Blacks in attendance, and I reluctantly realized that the well-meaning eyes, demeanors, and dominant demographics of my colleagues facilitated a type of PTSD in me, and I surmised in them, too. For the first time, I started to confront the unlikelihood of me being in *that space*. I was not supposed to be there, and if my conference colleagues acknowledged me in any substantive way, I would actually pop-materialize their (read: dominant) reality. (Isn't there some fable that if one doesn't believe in fairies, they cease to exist? It was like that.) So rather than confront the stressors that the social contradiction of the very presence of my Black female body in *that space* created, the dominant collective, subconsciously or consciously, decided that I was not there.[2] I couldn't be there; thus it was like sci-fi movie magic: poof! Now you see me; now you don't. (Much like a Ferengi Cloaking Device.) Jazz hands, and I'm gone!

---

2. "It is important to understand that the perpetrators of racial microaggession often unconsciously engage in microaggressive acts and thus can commit the act with little thought or attention paid to the interaction. . . . the unconscious intent of perpetrators make confronting microaggressions difficult for People of Color, and is one way racism can be perpetuated while rendered invisible" (13). See Lindsay Perez Huber and Daniel G. Solorzano, "Racial Microaggressions as a Tool for Critical Race Research," *Race Ethnicity and Education* 18, no. 3 (2015): 1–24.

So what happens when a group's actual invisibility, which can also be read as an absence or failure, is normalized, subsequently making that very invisibility central to maintaining a larger structural reality of dominant Whiteness within institutional spaces? What departments and their institutions are constantly trying to place the *Other* back into the *places* and *spaces* (the trauma) that they thought they had survived by failing to recognize the micro- and macro-aggressions experienced by the Other within the writing classroom, faculty spaces, and larger institution?

Have you taught at institutions where poor, Brown, and Black students consistently fail writing classes or fail to successfully matriculate through the institution over semesters and then over decades and respond and act as if *that* is normal? Do you have *that one Other* student, faculty, staff, and/or administrator, and you believe that your department/college is doing a great job at diversity? (To be read in a cheerleading voice, although I was a pom-pom girl not a cheerleader, as even here there is a hierarchy.) Do you teach at an institution where the demographics of the students and the communities that you serve are starkly different from the demographics of the faculty, staff, and administrators, and you believe that this is normal? Do you enter into a predominantly White classroom, faculty meeting, staff meeting, and/or administration leadership meeting and question if the racial makeup of the bodies in the room is equitable, or have you been desensitized and read the racial makeup of classrooms and other institutional spaces, if you even notice it at all, as normal? Do you even see it, or do you even want to see it?

What does it do to the teaching and acquisition of writing when the experiences and identities of the Other are silenced physically and intellectually through the complicity of the very people who consciously claim (for example, through assigned readings and office and hallway posters of equitable writers) to support equity and inclusion? How can racial equity exist in writing instruction and student outcomes when equity does not exist among those faculty who teach writing or within the institutions that house and serve them? What more explicit evidence of the historical legacy and contemporary status of the violent impacts of structural racism and its cumulative barriers is there than to enter into writing classrooms and other educational spaces and confront identity disparities, either through the actual disproportionate absence and/or presence of certain bodies relative to other bodies and/or the disproportionate, repeated, and patterned failure of certain students in writing classrooms and programs? To rationalize the disparity, consciously and subconsciously, is to actively perpetuate racism.

I get it, and I am compassionate. When Columbia, South Carolina police officer Ben Fields, a grown-ass man, "grabs . . . [a Black female] student by the neck, flipping her backward as she sat at her desk, then dragging and throwing her across the floor," it's much easier to cue the elevator music and wonder why, what happened, and to patiently ask and to be "deeply concerned" for the facts first, then to actually believe, accept, and to take action regarding the daily physical, mental, and emotional realities, literally and analogically, for marginalized bodies within classrooms and other institutional spaces.[3] I was not supposed to be a successfully matriculated college student, a college graduate, and a writing and literature teacher looking for a tenure-track faculty position. If I am not supposed to be there through the continued normalization of racially constructed and dominantly White spaces, places, and teaching positions, then who, too, is still not socially, historically, and institutionally constructed to be in the writing and/or literature classrooms? I

---

3. See Richard Fausset and Ashley South Hall, "Video Shows Officer Flipping Student in South Carolina, Prompting Inquiry," *New York Times*, October 26, 2015. Also, thepostfk, "Refreshing Elevator Music," YouTube.

guess I got out of Fields's chokehold and off the floor (so I think), but there are countless others still not able to fully breathe.

I teach at a local college where the majority of my writing department colleagues (all excellent, well-meaning, well-intentioned, and good people) are institutionally constructed as White, but the majority of the students and the communities that we and the college serve are poor and of color. As in many writing programs and their institutions in which they are housed, the matriculation rate for students of color is challenging, and there are structural issues with the recruitment and retention of faculty of color. Although we (Brown, Black, poor, and gendered bodies) are in the classrooms and the institution, our marginalized bodies are systematically subjected to macroaggressions, institutional racism, and racial microaggressions.[4] It is the failure of those with power and privilege within the discipline and the institution to actually look, see, recognize, and act to change historical and now contemporary patterns of exclusion of which we are all a part and perpetuate, consciously and unconsciously. This willful ignorance continues the systemic oppression of Brown, Black, poor, and gendered bodies on every finger and thumb of the institution's hand: the students in the classroom, the faculty instructors, the staff, the administration, and the communities that the college serves.

In the writing department, I have witnessed faculty of color and their White allies (metaphorically flipped out of their institutional chairs) be accused of being noncollegial, incompetent, intimidating, angry, racist, and bullies because they have attempted to address issues of equity and the intersections of identity and experience as it relates to curriculum, pedagogy, student success, and faculty of color recruitment and retention. These disparaging and unprofessional insults and labels have become the subsequent

---

4. See Huber and Solorzano, "Racial Microaggresions."

consequences of those who dare to see constructed Black and other marginalized identities and bodies and their experiences within the discipline of writing instruction and the larger academic institutions in which they are housed. Subsequently, these microaggression experiences of faculty of color mirror the experiences of students of color in writing classes and within the larger college, and they also mirror the recruitment, retention, and experiences of staff and administrators of color within the college.[5]

Walking around the conference and seeing my well-meaning and well-intentioned constructed White colleagues gave me flashbacks to my first-year composition class, when I was a first-generation student from Chicago's South Side attending a predominantly White public university in the Midwest. My well-meaning and well-intentioned White first-year composition teacher consistently told me, in her written feedback and final grade assessment of my paper assignments, that she could not understand what I was writing because it did not make any sense. Usually, I wrote about what I knew, which was being female, Black, poor, urban, and a first-time college student, away from home, attending a predominantly White college in the middle of the Midwest. Eventually, someone like Officer Fields was not called to the classroom, but I stopped attending class, and I failed my college composition course, although some of the essays were being published in campus-wide publications. A year later, after failing first-year composition like most students within my identity intersections, I dropped out of college. It would take five years before I would develop the courage and opportunity to return, let alone retake first-year writing. Sixteen years after completing my bachelor's degree, I can still walk into

5. "There are various types of microaggressions People of Color experience, based on race and/or ethnicity, gender, class, language, sexuality, immigration status, phenotypes, accent, surname, and/or culture," Kolhi and Solorzano, quoted in Huber and Solorzano, "Racial Microaggressions."

institutional venues for educators, and the educators are and were still primarily socially, historically, and institutionally constructed White and no one seems or seemed uncomfortable or aware. This constructed and dominant Whiteness in the field and discipline has been and is still completely normalized.

If we as teachers of writing normalize (read: accept) the dominant presence of constructed Whiteness in the field and discipline among our students and colleagues, how might that consciously and/or unconsciously affect our teaching in the classroom and the assessment of students? What is the constructed identity of our students who are prepared for college writing and who successfully matriculate through our college writing classrooms? Is it that these numbers reflect a reality or reflect a constructed reality that we, being liberal, well-meaning, and well-intentioned educators, help to construct? Do we merely watch, show concern, and amass facts and other data? How might educators, writing instruction programs, and institutions work to get up from up under this social, historical, and institutional bias that we have inherited through no fault of our own?

In response, I suggest the following steps as a start, not an absolute solution, toward equity in our classrooms and institutions:

- Fully understand what silence (lack of accountable, consistent, and transparent action) conveys.

- Avoid rationalization. There can only be one or two outcomes: either the failure of people of color and their infinite intersecting identities are normal inside and outside of the classroom, or there are institutional barriers that have prevented their very presence and success in the actual spaces that you and those of us with privilege inhabit.

- Don't ask and expect those who are the most institutionally and historically vulnerable among you to do the actual work of equity. The power of leading (big word) "equity" must reside within the leadership of the institution and must be embedded within its core cultural and institution-wide commitment, i.e., real, documented, and accountable pervasive policies and practices. If not, those who do equity work where there is no demonstrated and documented institutional commitment become sacrifices like lamb to be slaughtered.

- There must be some other oversight body, which then has the power of holding individual institutions and instructors transparently accountable when equity situations are dire; this is not a system of blaming, but don't just dance and listen to the orchestra while the *Titanic* is slowly sinking. This does not mean that individual programs are not free to construct their models relative to the communities and students that they serve, but to assume that individuals, who are well meaning and well intentioned, can autonomously maintain equity without a transparent checks-and-balance system in the face of decades and sometimes centuries of exclusion is to underestimate (ignore) the legacy and power of structural and institutional unconscious and conscious racism and bias.[6]

- If you are in any space or room where there is a dominant majority, don't normalize their presence or lack

---

6. Good times! For example, see the swift and subsequent suppression of voter rights in U.S. states after the Supreme Court struck down key provisions in the Voting Rights Act. See Gabrielle Levy, "Congress Moves to Restore Cuts Supreme Court Made to Voting Rights Act," *U.S. News & World Report*, June 24, 2015.

thereof and ignore it; ask yourself what social, historical, and institutional actions might have happened
that may have affected people directly and personally,
which prevented them from being in that (read: your)
time and space.

- Commit to working toward dismantling institutional and structural inequity as an institutional goal
  (practice)—mission statement, hiring practices, curriculum development and assessment—and permeate it
  throughout the body and life of the institution.

- Recognize that institutional consequences are disproportionate for the same institutional actions. Because
  of cumulative and historical and structural inequities,
  any institutional practice that disparages any member
  works to disparage the more vulnerable members of an
  institution even more.

- As has been said numerous times in many other places,
  inequity is the canary in the coal mine. Recognize that
  achieving equity benefits *all* members of the institution
  and the communities that we serve.

The demographics of that conference space, like the spaces of my
first-year composition course, our classrooms, our departments,
our conference spaces, and our larger institutions, did not just
happen. They are a result of the cumulative legacies of violent,
historical, contemporary, and ongoing institutional exclusion and
oppression. We will never get it right in these spaces until we first
understand, acknowledge, respect, and synthesize this historical
reality into our work, at every level, moving forward collectively.

Sometimes I Feel like Harriet Tubman

I was invited to speak at a Twin Cities area school, and it wasn't until I arrived at the school that the administrator asked me to discuss the immediate challenges facing parents and children in education in Minnesota.

Initially, I was hesitant because I didn't know if I wanted to take a personal risk with the topic. Sure, I could talk about literature, culture, and creative writing, but K-12 education in Minnesota is a sensitive topic freighted with anger, shame, and blame on all sides. And with my own three kids attending Twin Cities area schools, I have skin in the game.

According to the *New York Times*, "Black students [nationally] are suspended three times as often as their white peers; in Minnesota, it is eight times as often." Another report pointed out that while Black students are 41 percent of the student population in Minneapolis, they make up 76 percent of the suspensions.[1] Even the best quests for solutions on this issue are mired in the fact that racial disparities in Minnesota are some of the starkest in the nation.

---

1. Erica L. Green, "Why Are Black Students Punished So Often? Minnesota Confronts a National Quandary," *New York Times*, March 18, 2018. www.nytimes.com/2018/03/18/us/politics/school-discipline-disparities-white-black-students.html.

A Brown parent, a mother, at the back of the room stood and asked, "Can you give an example of implicit bias that has affected your own child in school?"

Her question forced me out of the autopilot zone that most professionals slip into when our hubris is set on high.

"That's a good question," I said, buying time.

Looking at the mother, I recognized that her mother body, like many weary parent bodies in the room, was seemingly at ease but conditioned to brace at any moment for the dreaded expected *unexpected*. I recognized my own mother body and experience inside hers. This is what it feels like to be the parent of a child in Minnesota schools who is the victim of implicit bias. Powerless.

I told the audience about my Black children who attend schools in the Twin Cities. Like their momma, they have dark brown skin with beautiful tightly curled hair. They are physically bigger than their classroom peers, and their speech reflects a confidence and experience beyond their years as they hear two different languages at home. Natural leaders, my Black children are kind and charming, and like their Tanzanian Bibi (grandmother) who is a lawyer working for the rights of women and children, my Black children are intelligent, smart, competitive, analytical, and protective. They have a keen sense of fairness and speak up if they sense inequity.

These unique qualities that make my Black children great are the very same qualities that are perceived by some teachers and administrators as aggressive, adult, disrespectful, loud, and defensive.

I laughed and told the mother that as the parent of children experiencing implicit bias, I often feel like Harriet Tubman on the Underground Railroad, trying to help my marginalized children get free, get educated. I added that my husband and I feel incredible fear and guilt at the recognition that our own educational success does not protect the Brown bodies of our children from the consequences of implicit bias within Minnesota schools.

"Yes. That's just how it feels," she said to me.

In that moment, with those amazing and hopeful parents who had cared enough to show up, I had no choice but to do what most well-meaning professionals in education fail to do: validate the experiences of non-White students and their parents, so we all know that we are not alone. We are not the only ones struggling with this very real educational and human rights crisis. And there is strength, hope, and healing in telling our stories.

Acknowledgments

I give gratitude and thanks to Source, the Ancestors, my Spirit Guides, and my intersecting communities for their creations, bravery, tenacity, sacrifices, guidance, protections, love, acceptance, expectations, and contributions to my life and this book.

Thank you to the editors who selected various content of this book for previous publications: Walter R. Jacobs, Wendy Thompson, Reshmi Dutt Ballerstadt, Kakali Bhattacharya, Patrick Sullivan, Shannon Gibney, Kao Kalia Yang, Sherry Quan Lee, Sun Yung Shin 신 선 영, Kathryn Kysar, Josh Wallaert, and Jennifer Vogel.

I thank my best friend and husband, Emmanuel (my babies' daddy), and our kids: Shose, Ellykunda, and Mirai, and our cat, Paka, for your love, support, and joy. I love you so much and am so grateful for the gifts of y'all in my life.

Thank you to my mother, father, baby brother, and three sisters (the Ten Tre); free government block cheese; cinnamon, sugar, and butter sandwiches; Double Dutch jump rope; and the small brown paper bags full of red wine Jolly Ranchers, candy cigarettes, and penny candy. I love you, Coleman and Boston crews!

My deepest gratitude to my teachers and mentors in this world and beyond for your empathy, compassion, work, instruction, wisdom, and generosity of your time and kindness that have and continue to support and inspire my voice and work: Alexs D. Pate, Donald Ross, Rose Brewer, Rosemary Olds, Mardell Oakley, David

Palmer, Omise'eke Natasha Tinsley, David Mura, Maria Damon, John Wright, Michael S. Harper, Karla Davis, Toi Derricotte, Rohan Preston, Angela Shannon, Kiese Laymon, David Lawrence Grant, Lucille Clifton, George Jackson, Linda and John Hagge, Mary Swander, Cornelius Eady, Carolyn and Sarah Micklem, Roderick Ferguson, Louis Moore, Debra Marquart, Wesley Brown, Linda Myers, Qadri Ismail, and Nikky Finney.

Thank you to Cave Canem and VONA for creating safe spaces and opportunities to write into myself a home.

Thank you to the Loft Literary Center.

Thank you to the McKnight Foundation.

Thank you to the Mellon Foundation.

Thank you to Ronald E. McNair and the TRIO program.

Thank you to the Archie Givens, Sr. Collection of African American Literature.

Thank you to Mapping Prejudice and your entire Jedi Knight team!

Thank you to St. Catherine University and *Welcoming the Dear Neighbor?*.

Thank you to Minneapolis College.

Thank you to the New Rivers Press: Many Voices Project for selecting content from this book as a prose manuscript book contest finalist in 2019.

Thank you, Nikki Giovanni, for writing that "Black love is Black wealth."

Thank you to Prince Rogers Nelson for being; Earth, Wind and Fire for writing "Truth is written in the stone"; and Stevie Wonder for "As."

Thank you, Zora Neale Hurston, for saying "If you are silent about your pain, they'll kill you and say you enjoyed it!"

Because it is truly an honor and privilege to do what you love and to continually learn and grow from it, I thank all my students (the real teachers) and those students (even more new real teachers) who will come.

Because we were probably practicing witchcraft together in a previous lifetime or right now in a simultaneously existing parallel dimension and messed some serious stuff up and we had to come back again to get it right or at least try to do it better while our paths crossed, I thank Kathleen Sheerin DeVore, Renee and Laura De-Long, Sun Yung Shin 신 선 영, Sherry Quan Lee, Milton McGriff, Willie Mitchell, Allan Nosworthy, Ánh-Hoa Thị Nguyễn, Andrea Jenkins, Valérie Déus, Bao Phi, Jared Santek, Lori Young-Williams, Derrick Lindstrom, Kristine Gyolai, Natalie Eschenbaum, Ebony Adams, D'Ann Urbaniak Lesch, Kel Munger, Kate Green, Sharon Doherty, Michael Kuhne, Kirsten Delegard, Tasha and Tong Pham, Robert (Bob) Grunst, Suzanne Lehman, Sekou Robertson, Nancy Heitzeg, and Erica Wallace Moore.

Thank you to the University of Minnesota Press, to Louisa Castner for magical copy editing, and to my editor, Erik Anderson, for the trust, opportunity, and patience to do this heavy lifting into the light together and for knowing about and loving Chicago House Music, Chicago Pizza Puffs and hot dogs, and that red is a color and also a flavor of pop.

References

The Thenar Space

Brazile, Donna, Yolanda Caraway, Leah Daughtry, and Minyon Moore. *For Colored Girls Who've Considered Politics*. New York: Macmillan, 2019.

Collins, Patricia Hill. *Black Feminist Thought*. New York: Routledge, 2009.

Douglass, Frederick. *The Narrative of the Life of Frederick Douglass: An American Slave Written by Himself*. New York: Bedford/St. Martin's Press, 1993.

Harris-Perry, Melissa V. "Crooked Room." In *Sister Citizen: Shame, Stereotypes, and Black Women in America*. New Haven, Conn.: Yale University Press, 2011.

Hughes, Langston. "The Negro Artist and the Racial Mountain." In *The Norton Anthology of African American Literature*, 2nd ed., ed. Henry Louis Gates and Nellie Y. McKay. New York: Norton, 2004.

Hugo, Richard. *The Triggering Town: Lectures and Essays on Poetry and Writing*. New York: Norton, 1979.

Hurston, Zora Neale. "Characteristics of Negro Expression." In *The Norton Anthology of African American Literature*, 2nd ed., ed. Henry Louis Gates and Nellie Y. McKay. New York: Norton, 2004.

King, Stephen. *On Writing: A Memoir of the Craft*. New York: Scribner, 2010.

Wright, Richard. "Blueprint for Negro Writing." In *The Norton Anthology of African American Literature*, 2nd ed., ed. Henry Louis Gates and Nellie Y. McKay. New York: Norton, 2004.

Fool's Gold

Landor, Antoinette M., et al. "Exploring the Impact of Skin Tone on Family Dynamics and Race-related Outcomes." *Journal of Family Psychology* 27, no. 5 (2013): 817–26. https://www.ncbi.nlm.nih.gov/pmc/articles/PMC3970169/.

Pirtle, Carol. "Andrew Borders v. William Hayes: Indentured Servitude and the Underground Railroad in Illinois." *Illinois Historical Journal* 89, no. 3 (Autumn 1996): 147–60.

Vonalt, Larry. "In the Heat of the Night." *Mississippi Encyclopedia* (Center for Study of Southern Culture), April 14, 2018.

Poems as a Mapping of Human Potential

Brand, Dionne. *A Map to the Door of No Return: Notes to Belonging*. Toronto: Doubleday Canada, 2001.

Clifton, Lucille. *good woman: poems and a memoir, 1969–1980*. Brockport, N.Y.: BOA Editions, 1987.

Lanham, J. Drew. "Compassing." https://placesjournal.org/article/compassing/.

Disparate Impacts

Douglass, Frederick. *The Narrative of the Life of Frederick Douglass: An American Slave Written by Himself*. New York: Bedford/St. Martin's Press, 1993.

Frohlich, Thomas C., et al., "The Worst States for Black Americans."
    24/7 Wall St., December 2, 2014. http://247wallst.com/special
    -report/2014/12/09/the-worst-states-for-black-americans/.

Mackenzie, John. "A Brief History of the Mason-Dixon Line." University of Delaware (2005). http://www.udel.edu/johnmack/
    mason_dixon/.

Wilkerson, Isabel. *The Warmth of Other Suns: The Epic Story of
    America's Great Migration.* New York: Vintage, 2010.

The Dangers of Teaching Writing While Black

Clementson, Lynette. "The Racial Politics of Speaking Well." *New
    York Times*, February 4, 2007.

Cutler, David. "Timeline: Liberia—from Civil War Chaos to Fragile Hope." *Reuters*, November 7, 2011.

Derrida, Jacques. "Difference." In *Margins of Philosophy*, trans.
    Alan Bass. Chicago: University of Chicago Press, 1984.

Freire, Paulo. *Pedagogy of the Oppressed.* New York: Penguin, 1996.

Gibney, Shannon. *Dream Country.* New York: Dutton, 2018.

"Liberian Refugees Have Earned the Right to Stay in U.S." *Star
    Tribune*, March 23, 2018. Editorial.

"Presidents of Liberia—in Chronological Order." *Liberia: Past and
    Present of Africa's Oldest Republic.* www.liberiapastandpresent
    .org.

Staples, Brent. "Just Walk On By: Black Men and Public Space."
    Harper's, December 1986. https://www.oleanschools.org/cms/
    lib/NY19000263/Centricity/Domain/166/Just%20Walk%20
    on%20By%20Black%20Men%20and%20Public%20Space.pdf.

Williams, Patricia J. *The Alchemy of Race and Rights: Diary of a Law
    Professor.* Cambridge, Mass.: Harvard University Press, 1992.

Wilson, Joseph IV. "Debunking Distortions about My Trip to
    Niger." *New York Times*, August 17, 2004.

What's Understood Don't Need to Be Explained

Coleman, Justine. "Texas Lt. Governor on Reopening State: 'There Are More Important Things Than Living.'" *The Hill*, April 21, 2020. thehill.com/homenews/state-watch/493879-texas-lt-gov ernor-on-reopening-state-there-are-more-important-things.

Eady, Cornelius. *Brutal Imagination: Poems*. New York: Penguin, 2001.

Grant, Kristin. "The History and Complexities of Gift Giving." *Reporter*, December 2, 2016. https://reporter.rit.edu/features/ history-and-complexities-gift-giving.

Jefferson, Thomas. Letter to John Holmes, April 22, 1820. Manuscript Division (159), Library of Congress (159). http://www .loc.gov/exhibits/jefferson/159.html.

Lisi, Brian. "Campus Security Guard Admits He Accidentally Shot Himself After First Lying about Black Man in a Hoodie with 'Short Afro.'" *New York Daily News*, September 14, 2017. https://www.nydailynews.com/news/crime/campus-guard -admits-shot-lying-black-man-article-1.3497871.

Patterson, Orlando. *Slavery and Social Death: A Comparative Study*. Cambridge, Mass.: Harvard University Press, 1982.

Pheifer, Pat. "St. Catherine University Security Officer Shot, Injured in St. Paul," *Star Tribune*, September 13, 2017. https:// www.startribune.com/security-officer-shot-on-st-kate-s-campus/ 444100363/.

Raddatz, Kate. "College Guard Who Shot Himself, Blamed 'Black Man,' Released from Jail." *CBS Minnesota*, September 14, 2017.

Siegel, Rachel. "A White Security Officer Told Police He Was Shot by a Black Man. Turns Out He'd Shot Himself," *Washington Post*, September 15, 2017. https://www.washingtonpost.com/news/ morning-mix/wp/2017/09/15/a-white-security-officer-told-police -he-was-shot-by-a-black-man-turns-out-hed-shot-himself/.

Xiong, Chao. "Ex-St. Catherine Guard Gets Probation for Making Up Story of Being Shot by a Black Man: Brent Ahlers Was Charged with Fabricating a Story of Being Shot by Black Man," *Star Tribune*, December 18, 2017. https://www.startribune.com/ex-st-catherine-guard-gets-probation-for-making-up-story-about-black-suspect/465030953/.

Xiong, Chao, and Paul Walsh. "NAACP Laments Wounded St. Kate's Security Officer Making Up Story about Black Gunman: NAACP Says Officer's False Shooter Story Rooted in Years of Racism in U.S," *Star Tribune*, September 14, 2017. https://www.startribune.com/wounded-st-kate-s-security-officer-who-lied-about-being-shot-said-gunman-was-black/444452013/.

Publication History

Essays published in this collection, here edited for consistency and stylistic tone, may vary slightly from earlier publications.

"The Thenar Space" was previously published as "The Thenar Space: Writing beyond Emotion and Experience into Story," in *How Dare We! Write: A Multicultural Creative Writing Discourse*, 2nd ed., edited by Sherry Quan Lee (Ann Arbor, Mich.: Modern History Press, 2022).

"Fool's Gold" was previously published as "Fool's Gold: On Looking, Seeing, and Feeling Ancestors and Their Stories of Survival as Mentorship," in Walker Art Center's *Mentors and Muses Series*, edited by Kao Kalia Yang. February 3, 2023. https://mnartists.walkerart.org/fools-gold.

"Grown Folks' Business" was previously published in *Riding Shot Gun: Women Writing about Their Mothers*, edited by Kathryn Kysar (St. Paul: Borealis Books, 2008), 41–54.

"Poems as a Mapping of Human Potential" was previously published as "Poems as Maps: An Introduction to the Series," *Places Journal* (August 2017).

"Disparate Impacts: Moving to Minnesota to Live Just Enough for the City" was published as "Disparate Impacts: Living Just Enough for the City," in *A Good Time for the Truth: Race in Minnesota,* edited by Sun Yung Shin (St. Paul: Minnesota Historical Society Press, 2016), 25–42.

"The Dangers of Teaching Writing While Black" was published as "Literacy and the Project of Killing the Black Body," in *Working toward Racial Equity in First-Year Composition: Six Perspectives* by Taiyon J. Coleman, Renee Delong, Kathleen Sheerin DeVore, Shannon Gibney, Michael C. Kuhne, and Valerie Deus (London: Taylor & Francis, 2019).

"Tilted Uterus: When Jesus Is Your Baby Daddy" was published in *What God Is Honored Here? Infant Loss by and for Native Women and Women of Color,* edited by Shannon Gibney and Kao Kalia Yang (Minneapolis: University of Minnesota Press, 2019), 45–65.

"Making the Invisible Visible: Mapping Racial Housing Covenants in South Minneapolis" was published as "Making the Invisible Visible: Mapping Racial Housing Covenants in South Minneapolis as a Cognitive Way to Improve Our Understanding of Structural Racism," *Minnesota Alumni Magazine,* Spring 2018.

"What's Understood Don't Need to Be Explained" was published as "What's Understood Don't Need to Be Explained: Sometimes Gifts Come in Ugly Packages," in *Sparked: George Floyd, Racism, and the Progressive Illusion,* edited by Walter R. Jacobs, Wendy Thompson Taiwo, and Amy August (St. Paul: Minnesota Historical Society Press, 2021), 77–83.

"You Can Miss Me with That, 'Cause Plantations Were Diverse, Too" was published as "You Can Miss Me with That, 'Cause Plantations Were Diverse, Too: A Personal Narrative as a Window to Possible Strategies for Supporting and Engaging Equity in Writing Instruction and Institutional Transformation," in Act V as my contribution to the larger article "The Risky Business of Engaging Racial Equity in Writing Instruction: A Tragedy in 5 Acts," by Taiyon J. Coleman, Renee DeLong, Kathleen Sheerin DeVore, Shannon Gibney, and Michael Kuhne (May 2016). My essay was also reprinted in *16 Teachers Teaching: Two-Year College Perspectives*, edited by Patrick Sullivan (Logan: Utah State University Press, 2020), 168–200.

"Sometimes I Feel like Harriet Tubman" was published in *Minnesota Alumni Magazine*, Fall 2018.

Taiyon J. Coleman is associate professor of literature, language, and writing, and gender and women's studies, at St. Catherine University in St. Paul, Minnesota. She also teaches writing at Minneapolis College. She holds degrees in English and English literature from Iowa State University and in creative writing and English literature and culture, with a minor in African American and African diaspora studies, from the University of Minnesota, where she was an Archie Givens, Sr. Collection of African American Literature Research Fellow.